Collins

YOUR CHOICE

BOOK ONE

JOHN FOSTER & SIMON FOSTER

Collins

William Collins' dream of knowledge for all began with the publication of his first book in 1819.

A self-educated mill worker, he not only enriched millions of lives, but also founded a flourishing publishing house. Today, staying true to this spirit, Collins books are packed with inspiration, innovation and practical expertise. They place you at the centre of a world of possibility and give you exactly what you need to explore it.

Collins. Freedom to teach.

Published by Collins

An imprint of HarperCollins*Publishers*

The News Building
1 London Bridge Street
London
SE1 9GF

HarperCollins*Publishers*
1st Floor, Watermarque Building, Ringsend Road
Dublin 4, Ireland

Browse the complete Collins catalogue at
www.collins.co.uk

© HarperCollins*Publishers* Limited 2019

10 9 8 7 6

ISBN 978-0-00-832897-9

British Library Cataloguing in Publication Data

A catalogue record for this publication is available from the British Library.

The publishers would like to thank the following for their help in reviewing the series:
- Jo Fliski, formerly Head of PSHE and English teacher at Lliswerry High School, Newport
- Jo Haycock, Psychology teacher at Sir John Talbot's School, Whitchurch, Shropshire and formerly PSHE Coordinator at Newport Girls' High School
- Tara Mellor, teacher of PSHE, Citizenship and Law, The Mirfield Free Grammar and Sixth Form.
- Cat Crossley, diversity consultant and publisher.

Development editor: Jo Kemp
Series editor: John Foster
Commissioning editor: Catherine Martin
Copyeditor: Jo Kemp
Proofreader: Emily Hooton
Cover designer: The Big Mountain
Concept designer: The Big Mountain
Internal designer / Typesetter: 2Hoots Publishing Services Ltd
Illustrations by Jouve India Ltd and Ken Vail Graphic Design
Permissions researcher: Rachel Thorne Production controller: Katharine Willard

MIX
Paper from
responsible sources
FSC™ C007454

This book is produced from independently certified FSC paper to ensure responsible forest management.

For more information visit: **www.harpercollins.co.uk/green**

Printed and bound in the UK using 100% Renewable Electricity at CPI Group (UK) Ltd

Contents

Introduction

Your Choice Book 1 is the first of three books which together form a comprehensive course in Personal, Social and Health Education (PSHE), including Relationships and Sex Education (RSE) and Health Education, at Key Stage 3. The table shows how the topics covered fit within four strands – Personal wellbeing and mental health, Relationships and sex education, Physical health and wellbeing and Social education – and could provide a coherent course for students in Year 7. Each unit could also be taught on its own, at any point during Key Stage 3 that your school thinks is appropriate.

The units provide you with key information on relevant topics, and the various activities provide opportunities for you to share your views and to develop your own opinions.

Throughout the book there are discussion activities that involve you in learning how to work as a team and how to develop the skills of co-operation and negotiation. You are presented with situations in which you have to work with others, to analyse information, to consider what actions you could take and to make choices and decisions.

Personal wellbeing and mental health

These units focus on developing your self-knowledge and self-awareness, including how you manage your emotions and make responsible decisions.

1 You and your identity
3 You and your feelings – anxieties and worries
4 You and your values
10 You and your decisions
15 You and your feelings – managing emotions
16 You and your money
17 You and your leisure

Relationships and sex education

These units focus on puberty, your rights and responsibilities in your relationships, protection and contraception, and keeping safe on the internet.

2 You and your changing body
5 You and other people
6 You and your knowledge about sex
7 You and your relationships
8 You and bullying
9 You and the internet

Each lesson has a clear focus.

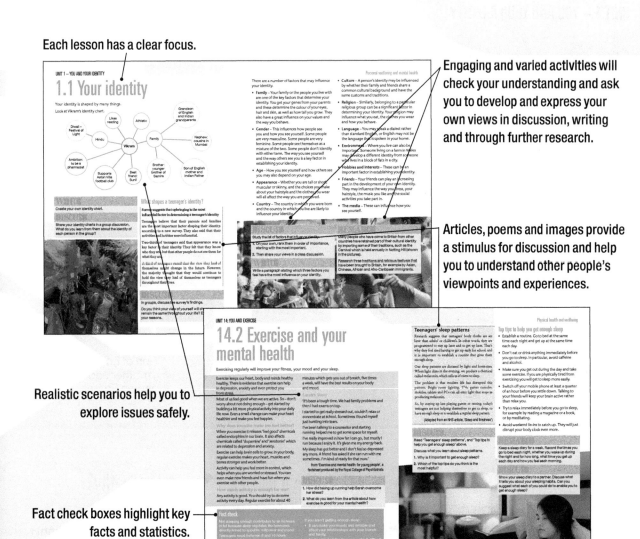

Engaging and varied activities will check your understanding and ask you to develop and express your own views in discussion, writing and through further research.

Articles, poems and images provide a stimulus for discussion and help you to understand other people's viewpoints and experiences.

Realistic scenarios help you to explore issues safely.

Fact check boxes highlight key facts and statistics.

Physical health and wellbeing

These units focus on those things that most affect your physical health and wellbeing, including drugs, diet, exercise, smoking and a section on first aid.

11   You and smoking
12   Drugs and drug taking
13   You and your diet
14   You and exercise
20   You and first aid

Social education

These units focus on your values and attitudes towards other people in society. They will help you to express your opinions and understand how to be a good neighbour.

18   You and your opinions
19   You and the local community

1.1 Your identity

Your identity is shaped by many things.

Look at Vikram's identity chart.

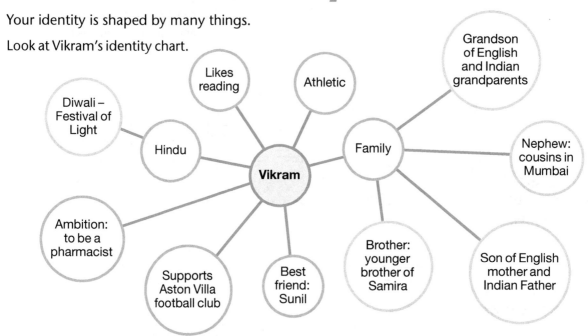

WRITE

Create your own identity chart.

DISCUSS

Share your identity charts in a group discussion. What do you learn from them about the identity of each person in the group?

What shapes a teenager's identity?

Survey suggests that upbringing is the most influential factor in determining a teenager's identity

Teenagers believe that their parents and families are the most important factor shaping their identity, according to a new survey. They also said that their activities and hobbies were influential.

Two-thirds of teenagers said that appearance was a key factor in their identity. They felt that they know who they are, but that other people do not see them for what they are.

A third of teenagers stated that the view they had of themselves might change in the future. However, the majority thought that they would continue to hold the view they had of themselves as teenagers throughout their lives.

DISCUSS

In groups, discuss the survey's findings.

Do you think your view of yourself will change or remain the same throughout your life? Explain your reasons.

There are a number of factors that may influence your identity.

- **Family** – Your family or the people you live with are one of the key factors that determine your identity. You get your genes from your parents and these determine the colour of your eyes, hair and skin, as well as how tall you grow. They also have a great influence on your values and the way you behave.

- **Gender** – This influences how people see you and how you see yourself. Some people are very masculine. Some people are very feminine. Some people see themselves as a mixture of the two. Some people don't identify with either term. The way you see yourself and the way others see you is a key factor in establishing your identity.

- **Age** – How you see yourself and how others see you may also depend on your age.

- **Appearance** – Whether you are tall or short, muscular or skinny, and the choices you make about your hairstyle and the clothes you wear will all affect the way you are perceived.

- **Country** – The country in which you were born and the country in which you live are likely to influence your identity.

- **Culture** – A person's identity may be influenced by whether their family and friends share a common cultural background and have the same customs and traditions.

- **Religion** – Similarly, belonging to a particular religious group can be a significant factor in determining your identity. Your religion may influence what you eat, the clothes you wear and how you behave.

- **Language** – You may speak a dialect rather than standard English, or English may not be the language that is spoken in your home.

- **Environment** – Where you live can also be important. Someone living on a farm in Wales may develop a different identity from someone who lives in a block of flats in a city.

- **Hobbies and interests** – These can be an important factor in establishing your identity.

- **Friends** – Your friends can play an increasing part in the development of your own identity. They may influence the way you dress, your hairstyle, the music you like and the social activities you take part in.

- **The media** – These can influence how you see yourself.

DISCUSS

Study the list of factors that influence identity.

1. On your own, rank them in order of importance, starting with the most important.
2. Then share your views in a class discussion.

WRITE

Write a paragraph stating which three factors you feel have the most influence on your identity.

RESEARCH

Many people who have come to Britain from other countries have retained part of their cultural identity by importing some of their traditions, such as the Carnival which is held annually in Notting Hill (shown in the pictures).

Research three traditions and religious festivals that have been brought to Britain, for example by Asian, Chinese, African and Afro-Caribbean immigrants.

1.2 Your personality

Your personality is a combination of all the qualities that make up your character. For example, you may be easy-going and laid-back, or you may be anxious and conscientious. Whatever qualities you have determine your personality.

Nature or nurture?

Your personality is the result of two main factors: the characteristics you inherit from your parents and the environment in which you are brought up. Experts disagree about which of these two factors is more important. Is your behaviour due more to your genes or to your upbringing?

As you grow up and face new challenges and choices, so you may develop new qualities.

Your personality influences how you behave, so it is important to understand what qualities you have.

DISCUSS

What sort of person are you?

1. On your own, study the list of words below and decide which five best describe your character.

2. Then choose a partner and write down the five words which best describe their character.

3. Show your partner the two lists and discuss any differences. What do the lists tell you about your personality and your partner's personality?

adventurous ambitious anxious bossy caring cautious cheerful considerate conscientious courageous courteous dependable easy-going faithful funny hardworking honest imaginative loyal modest optimistic patient pessimistic practical quick-tempered reliable selfish serious shy stubborn sympathetic tactful tidy unselfish

Remember, though, your personality is not the only factor that influences your behaviour. The way you behave is also influenced by what is going on in your life. For example, you may be under stress because of a family situation or feel under pressure from your peers to behave like them.

DISCUSS

1. On your own, decide how you would react in each of the situations described below.

2. Discuss with a partner what this tells you about your personality.

Situation 1

You are at a theme park. Your friend wants to go on the big dipper but you are frightened. Do you agree to go on with them? What does your decision say about you?

Situation 2

You are offered a ticket to a football match on a day when you have promised to go out with your best friend. You want to go to the match. What do you decide to do? What does the way you react say about you? How would you feel if you were the friend and were being let down? If you were the friend, what would you do?

Situation 3

You are not selected for the team that's going to play in the final. How do you react? What does your reaction say about you?

Situation 4

You fail an important test. What do you do? Do you pretend it doesn't matter or make up your mind to do better next time? What does your reaction tell you about yourself?

Situation 5

You see someone being picked on and called names during break. What do you do?

Are you an introvert or an extrovert?

There are two main types of personality: introverts and extroverts. Introverts focus on their own thoughts and feelings to get their energy. Extroverts are lively, friendly and enjoy being with other people. Whereas an extrovert enjoys social situations, an introvert may enjoy spending time on their own or with smaller groups of friends.

Most people are neither complete introverts nor complete extroverts. But it can be useful to understand your preferences.

Characteristics of an introvert	Characteristics of an extrovert
• Introverts tend to be shyer in social situations.	• Extroverts are outgoing and confident in social situations.
• They tend to be reserved and not to show outwardly what they are feeling.	• They tend to be open and to show their feelings.
• They are happy relaxing quietly on their own.	• They enjoy having lots of people around.
• They work well on their own.	• They work well in groups.
• They tend to listen more than they speak.	• They tend to speak more than they listen.
• They are less likely to volunteer their opinions unless asked to do so.	• They speak up in discussions and are keen to express their opinions.
• They are more likely to suffer from embarrassment.	• They are less embarrassed if they make mistakes.
• They are less likely to seek new experiences, and may struggle with change.	• They enjoy new experiences and accept change easily.
• They take time to reflect before making decisions.	• They make decisions quickly.
• They have closer relationships with a few friends.	• They have more friends, but have close relationships with fewer of them.
• They can concentrate well for a long time.	• They are easily distracted.

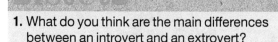

DISCUSS

1. What do you think are the main differences between an introvert and an extrovert?

2. What are you? Do you think you are more of an introvert or an extrovert?

WRITE

Write one or two paragraphs outlining what you have learned about your identity and your personality from this unit.

RESEARCH

Psychologists suggest that there are a number of common personality types. Find out about the different personality types by researching a theory known as the Enneagram. Which of the nine possible personality types do you most identify with?

1.3 Who am I?

An ethnic group is a group of people who share a common ancestry, religion, culture, language or society. Who you are depends on who your parents are, where you were born and where you live.

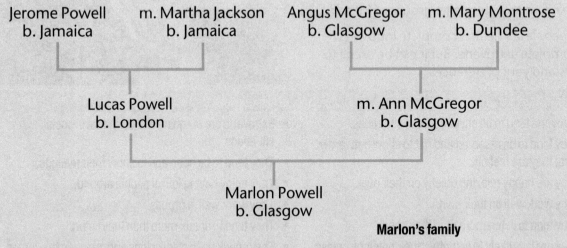

Jerome Powell
b. Jamaica   m. Martha Jackson
b. Jamaica   Angus McGregor
b. Glasgow   m. Mary Montrose
b. Dundee

Lucas Powell
b. London   m. Ann McGregor
b. Glasgow

Marlon Powell
b. Glasgow

Marlon's family

Jerome Powell came to England with his wife Martha in 1960. They were part of the Windrush generation of West Indians who came to Britain after World War Two. Their son, Lucas, followed them two years later when he was 6. Lucas went to school in London, then spent three years working in Glasgow, where he met and married Ann McGregor. They live in London and have a son, Marlon, who was born in Glasgow.

Jerome had two sisters and a brother who stayed in Jamaica, so Marlon has relatives in Jamaica as well as members of his mother's family in Scotland.

DISCUSS

1. List the ethnic groups that Marlon has in his background. How would you classify Marlon? Is he European? Jamaican? Scottish? Afro-Caribbean? British? Glaswegian? A Londoner?

2. What ethnic groups do you belong to? Talk about how there are people from many different backgrounds living in Britain today.

RESEARCH

1. Who were the Windrush generation?

2. Why did they come to Britain?

3. What was it about the Windrush generation that caused a public outcry in 2018, and what happened as a result?

You are a citizen of the country in which you are born, but you may be granted citizenship of another country if you have lived there for a number of years.

If you want to travel to any other country, you will need a passport. You can apply for a passport to be issued by the country in which you were born.

Some people have two passports – one for the country in which they were born and one for the country their parents come from. They are said to have dual nationality.

Alice was born in Australia. She has a British mother and an Australian father. When she was 5 years old her parents split up and she and her mother returned to England from Australia. Her mother wanted her to have British nationality as well as Australian nationality and applied for a British passport as well as an Australian one. So, Alice has two passports.

A large number of people choose to make their homes in another country rather than the country of their birth.

Others may have come as refugees or entered the country illegally. Some may be granted asylum and allowed to stay, while others may face deportation despite having lived in the United Kingdom for many years.

WRITE

'Anyone who has lived and worked legally in Britain for 5 years or more should be entitled to apply for British citizenship.'

Discuss this view in groups and then write a statement saying why you agree or disagree with it.

Read the poem 'Immigration Trap'.

Immigration Trap

Farida's mum is being sent home.
But Farida's allowed to stay.
Farida doesn't want her to go
But Farida doesn't have a say.

Farida's lived here all her life.
She's British, like you and me.
But Farida's mum came here
As a stateless refugee.

And now the people who make the rules
Say Farida's mum must go
Back to the land she left
Twelve long years ago.

Back to a troubled land
Where people live in fear.
She has outstayed her welcome.
She is not wanted here.

But because Farida was born here,
Farida's allowed to stay.
She doesn't want her mum to go,
But she doesn't have a say.

By John Foster

DISCUSS

1. Should Farida's mum be deported?

2. Should Farida have to go with her?

3. Should Farida be allowed to stay, provided there is someone to look after her?

4. Should there be an amnesty allowing people to stay in the UK who entered the country illegally but who have lived in the UK for ten years or more?

1.4 Gender and your identity

How far does your gender shape your identity?

Gender and sex are words that many people use interchangeably to describe differences between boys and girls, or males and females. In fact, the term 'sex' is a biological one referring to differences in our bodies and genetic make-up. Your sex is usually decided at birth. 'Gender' refers to the roles and behaviours that society suggests are normal for men and women. 'Gender identity' means how someone feels about or expresses their gender.

Gender development

Our sense of our own gender develops and changes during childhood. As we get older, we become more aware that we are expected to have certain interests and dress and behave in particular ways because of our gender.

Read the examples below.

'I am a tom-boy – my mum despairs of the fact that I don't want to wear 'girly' clothes and that I like climbing trees and playing football!'
Hannah, 11

'I often get teased at school because I dance – people don't expect boys to want to do ballet. I have always loved it, though, and I won't let anyone stop me.'
Tom, 12

'I love being a boy and doing things with my dad and his mates – going fishing together and playing football.'
Razvan, 13

DISCUSS

1. What kind of behaviours and interests are often associated with boys?

2. What kind of behaviours and interests are often associated with girls?

3. Are there some behaviours and interests that are equally associated with boys and girls?

4. Do you think this matters?

Stereotypes

Gender stereotypes are generalised beliefs about what each gender is like. You may have heard people suggesting we need to 'fight' these stereotypes. That is because they are often used negatively and can be limiting.

For example, if girls are thought to be more emotional than boys, it might be assumed they would not make good soldiers or be able to fight on the front line. Conversely, boys may be considered less suitable for caring roles such as working in a nursery.

Of course, a boy may be more caring than a girl. And a girl may be cooler under pressure than a boy. This is why stereotypes can be dangerous – they make assumptions whereas, we should treat each person as an individual.

Changing times

If you talk to parents, carers and grandparents, they will probably tell you how things have changed since they were young. In most UK schools today, for example, all children have the same choice of subjects to study. In many schools, girls are able to play traditionally male sports such as football or rugby and can wear trousers as part of their school uniform. Boys, too, can choose to study childcare, dance or other subjects that may have only been open to girls in the past. These are things we may take for granted now, but they have not always been this way.

RESEARCH

Ask a teacher, parent, grandparent or carer about how boys and girls were treated when they were growing up. Do you prefer the way things were or how they are now?

Challenging stereotypes

Many people believe that equality will involve all gender stereotypes being challenged, so that children are free to choose what they want to play with, wear, spend their time doing or become when they are older, without any feeling that they should or should not do something because of their gender.

One way in which gender stereotypes are being challenged is by a small number of parents who decide not to tell anyone the gender of their newborn baby.

When a baby is born the first question is usually, 'Is it a boy or girl?' So, what would your reaction be if you were told, 'We've decided not to say'? A small number of parents are now choosing this option.

These parents argue that gender 'labelling' restricts the opportunities of a child and affects the way that people act towards the child. For example, parents and carers have been seen to engage in more rough and tumble play with boys and to encourage calmer play with girls. Parents and carers may also choose different toys for boys and girls, which may in turn lead to the child developing particular interests or skills.

By choosing gender-neutral names like Jordan or Phoenix and by dressing children neutrally, the aim is to allow the children to explore their own identity and interests free from society's gender rules.

DISCUSS

1. What do you think of this idea?

2. What might happen when the child goes to school or begins to play with other children?

3. 'It is okay to be a girl who loves pink and plays with dolls, but it's just as okay for a girl to like football and video games. The same is true for boys. It's your choice.' Do you agree with this statement?

RESEARCH

Find out more online about bringing up a child as gender neutral.

When your gender doesn't feel right

Some young people's feelings about the sex they were given at birth go far beyond a desire to challenge gender stereotypes. Deep feelings of not being comfortable in their given gender can lead to a young person wanting to change their gender identity in some way. *Trans and non-binary gender identities are explored in more depth in Your Choice Book 3 Unit 2.*

2.1 Puberty

Puberty is the time of life when you develop from a child into an adult.

Growing and changing

Puberty usually starts around the age of 11 or 12 – although it can be earlier or later than this, so don't worry if your experience is different.

A group of 12 year olds were asked to say how they thought they had changed during the last 18 months.

How have you changed in the last 18 months?

1. 'I've put on weight so I'm much heavier, and I've grown taller too.'

2. 'I've got much hairier and my muscles have developed, so I'm much stronger.'

3. 'My hair is more greasy and I've got spots on my face.'

4. 'My voice is breaking. It swings from squeaky and high to very deep.'

5. 'My body shape has changed. I've started to develop breasts and I'm more curvy.'

6. 'I've started to have my periods.'

7. 'My mood changes often – sometimes I feel happy and excited and sometimes I feel down.'

8. 'I argue more with my parents.'

9. 'I want to make my own decisions, not have them made for me.'

10. 'I am more interested in sex.'

11. 'I want to have my own space. I get annoyed with anyone who comes into my room without being invited.'

12. 'I keep my thoughts more to myself and have more secrets.'

13. 'I get angry more easily and am easily embarrassed.'

DISCUSS

Discuss what each of the children says.

1. Which comments were probably made by girls?

2. Which comments were probably made by boys?

3. Which could have been made by both boys and girls?

Puberty: your questions answered

Q. *At what age does puberty start?*

A. Puberty occurs at different times for different people. So it's perfectly normal for puberty to begin at any age between 8 and 14, and to last for 2 to 5 years.

Q. *What causes puberty?*

A. The changes happen because of the sex hormones produced by the testicles in boys and by the ovaries in girls. Some of the changes are the same. For example, both boys and girls grow underarm hair and pubic hair. Their growth rate increases and they both experience emotional changes.

Q. *What other changes are there to boys' bodies?*

A. The penis and testicles get bigger. They begin to produce sperm. They grow hair on the face and chest. Their shoulders get wider. Their voice breaks and gets deeper. Boys may begin to have 'wet dreams'. These are dreams that cause a boy to get an erection and to ejaculate sperm during his sleep. He may not remember the dream and only realise that he has had one when he wakes up in the morning.

Q. *What other changes are there to girls' bodies?*

A. Their ovaries begin to release eggs and their periods start. Their breasts develop and their hips get wider.

Ask Erica

Dear Erica
I feel that I'm getting left behind by my friends. They all look so much more grown up than me. I've hardly started to develop at all. I'm shorter than all of them. I've got a bit of underarm hair but that's about it.
Christian

Dear Erica
I'm thirteen and I haven't started my periods yet. I'm the only one in my group of friends who hasn't. My mum tells me not to worry, but one of the group has started to tease me about it.
Eveline

WRITE

Draft Erica's replies to Christian and Eveline.

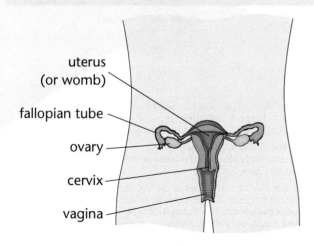

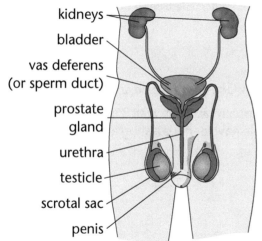

Thoughts and feelings

In addition to changes to your body, puberty brings changes to your thoughts and feelings.

- You may find it harder to talk to your parents or carers because you are developing your own ideas, values and opinions.
- You may be more self-conscious and feel shy and embarrassed in social situations.
- You may feel envious of people who are self-confident.
- You may want to spend more time alone.
- You may worry about your appearance.
- You may feel it is important to be identified as a member of a particular group and to have a particular hairstyle and/or wear the same clothes as that group.
- Your mood may swing from being extremely happy one moment to very sad the next.
- You may feel more anxious about things than you used to.
- You may feel angry because one moment you are expected to behave like an adult and the next you are treated like a child.

These thoughts and feelings are all part of the growing-up process.

Ask Erica

Dear Erica
I used to get on well with my parents, but lately I've been rowing with them. Sometimes I'm happy when I'm with them, but then suddenly I want to be alone. I'm so confused. Can you help me?
Ursula

WRITE

1. Draft Erica's reply to Ursula.

2. Write a question about puberty which you want to know the answer to. Put your question in the question box your teacher has put in the classroom. In the next lesson your teacher will answer the questions you have put in the box. The questions will be anonymous, so no one will know who asked which question.

2.2 Periods: the facts

For most girls, the first signs that they are entering puberty are that they grow taller and their breasts start to grow. A girl will usually get her first period a year or two later. But exactly when this will happen can vary a lot.

The first period shows that a girl's body has changed and that she is able to have a baby. When you have a period, you lose a small amount of blood through your vagina. This is called menstruating. Women continue to have periods regularly until they reach the menopause, which usually happens between the ages of 45 and 55 years.

What happens during a period?

Periods happen on a monthly cycle. Every month, one of the ovaries releases an egg, which travels down the fallopian tube to the uterus (womb). This is where a baby would grow if the egg were fertilised by a sperm, which can happen if you have sexual intercourse up to seven days before and one day after the egg is released. Sperm can survive inside a woman's body for up to seven days. If it is not fertilised, the egg travels down the womb and out of the body in the blood that you lose when you menstruate.

At first periods may not be regular, but eventually most women settle into a cycle of having a period every 28 to 30 days. However, it can vary from person to person, with some having longer or shorter cycles.

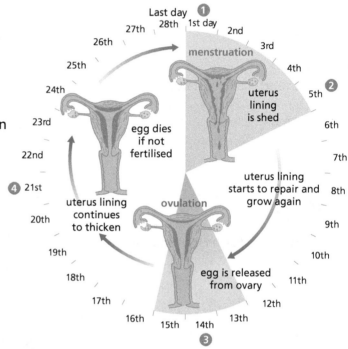

1. The first day of the cycle is when blood loss first occurs. The thick, blood-filled lining of the uterus breaks down and is lost through the vagina.

2. After about day 5, the lining builds up again, replenishing the uterus with blood and nutrients. An egg in the ovary begins to ripen.

3. At about day 14, hormones cause the egg to mature and ovulation to occur. The egg moves down the fallopian tube towards the uterus. The lining of the uterus has been building up and is now very thick, ready to receive a fertilised egg.

4. Three weeks into the cycle, and the egg has now reached the uterus – if it is unfertilised it will die.

Periods: your questions answered

Q. *Does it hurt when you have your period?*

A. Many girls get period pains or cramps in the lower abdomen, where the uterus is situated, during their period. The pain is caused by the uterus contracting as the lining is shed. Painkillers such as ibuprofen or paracetamol, exercise and having a warm bath or using a hot water bottle can ease the pain.

Q. *How long does a period last?*

A. It usually lasts between 3 and 5 days, but some people have periods lasting a week.

Q. *Which sanitary product should I use?*

A. It's up to you. Some girls prefer to use sanitary towels, and most use these when they first get their period. Others prefer tampons. Another option is the menstrual cup, which is a cup made of silicone which fits into the vagina and collects the blood rather than absorbing it.

Q. *What is premenstrual syndrome?*

A. Changes to the hormone levels in your body before your monthly period can cause some physical and emotional changes. These might include feeling bloated, breasts feeling tender, experiencing mood swings and feeling irritable. You may get more spots than usual and your hair may be greasier.

YOUR CHOICE

On your own, do this test-yourself quiz about periods. Decide which are facts and which are myths. Then compare your answers in a class discussion.

1. The length of a period can be anything from three days to a week.

2. A person is unclean when they are having their period.

3. Everyone can tell when you have your period.

4. You go on having periods throughout your adult life.

5. Girls are likely to be more emotional before their periods start.

6. You should not wash your hair when you have your period.

7. The menstrual cycle is the same for all girls and women.

8. You shouldn't do any exercise when you have your period.

9. You cannot become pregnant if you have sex during your period.

10. A girl who uses tampons isn't a virgin.

Tampon tax

Most girls use tampons and sanitary towels when they get their periods. However, the government has classed these as luxury goods, which means they are charged with a tax – VAT. This pushes up the cost of tampons by 5 per cent. Some female MPs have started a campaign in Parliament to get this tax removed. They argue that tampons are not a luxury for girls and young women – they are a necessity – and therefore the tax should be removed from them. Campaigners have even asked people to start donating tampons to food banks to help those who may be in 'period poverty'.

RESEARCH

Research online how the campaign to make tampons VAT-free is going, and whether or not your MP supports it.

Ask Erica

Dear Erica
One of my friends had an accident at school when her period came during a lesson. Some boys saw what had happened and started sniggering and making crude comments. One of them was my younger sister's boyfriend. What should I do?

Tess

WRITE

Draft Erica's reply to Tess.

3.1 Feeling worried or anxious

Everyone feels worried at some time, but what matters is being able to manage your anxiety.

What worries you?

'I worry about lots of things. Am I normal? Am I attractive? What do other people think of me?'

What makes you feel anxious?

1. 'I'm anxious about the trip we're going on to this outdoor activities centre. We're going to do rock climbing and I'm scared of heights.'

2. 'I'm the goalkeeper and our team has reached the final of the county cup. I'm worried I'll let the team down.'

3. 'Recently my parents have been rowing a lot. I'm worried they are going to split up.'

4. 'We've just moved and I'm going to a new school. I'm worried I won't make any friends.'

5. 'I'm worried that I haven't done enough revision and I won't do well in the tests.'

6. 'I'm really worried about the holiday they've booked. We're going to Cyprus by plane and I'm terrified of flying.'

7. 'I'm worried about going swimming and that everyone will stare at me because I'm overweight.'

8. 'I'm worried about people finding me unattractive because I've got to wear glasses.'

9. 'I'm worried about my grandpa. He's got Motor Neurone Disease.'

10. 'I'm worried about falling out with my friends because they went to the cinema together and I wasn't invited.'

11. 'There have been some break-ins in our street and I'm worried about going to sleep in case someone comes into our house.'

12. 'I'm worried that something has happened to our cat. We haven't seen her for five days.'

YOUR CHOICE

Some worries are more serious than others. On your own, use a scale of 1 to 10 to say how serious you think each of them is, with 10 being extremely serious.

Then compare your answers with a partner.

WRITE

Imagine that the 12 people who made these statements wrote to Erica, an agony aunt, asking for her advice. Choose two statements and draft Erica's replies to them.

Coping with worries and anxieties

There is an old saying, 'A worry shared is a worry halved'. The best thing to do is talk to someone. Sharing your worries will help to put them in perspective. It may also reveal the action you need to take, or where you need to go to get help.

Are you self-conscious?

Do you get anxious when you have to do things in front of other people? Are you self-conscious, or doesn't it bother you? Read the anxieties people have written to Erica about opposite and her answers to them.

Ask Erica

Dear Erica
I don't like it when I have to give a speech to the rest of the class.
Anthony

Erica says: It's natural to feel a bit anxious when there is pressure on you to do something you'd rather not do. But you'd be surprised to know that even the most experienced speakers get nervous before talking to an audience. Try to look calm and confident even though you don't feel it, and tell yourself that you can cope.

Dear Erica
I get tongue-tied when I meet friends of my parents.
Esme

Erica says: It can be difficult when you meet people you've never met before. Prepare some phrases that you can use like, 'Did you have a good journey?', 'Have you come far?' 'I'm very pleased to meet you.' Make 'small talk' to break the ice.

Dear Erica
I can't bear it when I make a mistake and everyone laughs at me.
Jared

Erica says: Don't worry! We all make mistakes, including the people who are laughing at you. Whatever you've done, try to see the funny side. If you can laugh at yourself, you can make the mistake less embarrassing.

Dear Erica
When I go into a room full of people I feel as if everyone is looking at me and judging me by how I look.
Veronica

Erica says: You may briefly be the centre of attention, but the chances are that you think more people are looking at you than actually are. The people are probably involved in conversations and, although they may glance in your direction, it will only be briefly.

Dear Erica
I'm embarrassed when people say things like, 'Haven't you grown', and 'I remember you when you were a baby'.
Robyn

Erica says: It's annoying, but it's not really important. You just have to put up with it – especially from elderly relatives, who usually mean well.

DISCUSS

Think about each of the people who have written to Erica. Discuss the questions below.

1. Can you understand why they feel anxious and self-conscious?

2. Do you think Erica gives good advice?

3. What further advice would you give them?

WRITE

Think about a time when you felt embarrassed and self-conscious. Write a couple of paragraphs about it.

- Explain how you dealt with the situation.

- Say how you handled it and whether you could have handled it better.

RESEARCH

When fear causes such anxiety that it stops someone from doing something, it is known as a phobia. Use the internet to find out about two or three common phobias, like the fear of spiders or flying, and how to deal with them.

3.2 The laws of attraction

What makes a person attractive is their personality not their looks.

Fact check

A survey of 1,500 young people aged 8 to 17 years old found that 84 per cent had shared a photo online.

Over half of them worried about how attractive they looked when they shared photos, and nearly half had used a filter to improve how they looked.

Am I attractive?

'Good looks aren't everything,'
says Trinia Newsome

As young people go through puberty, they become more aware of their appearance. They think about how they look and ask themselves if others will find them attractive.

They become more concerned become more concerned with their clothes and personal hygiene. They may experiment with hairstyles. How others see them matters.

When it comes to how attractive you are, good looks aren't the only thing that makes a person attractive. What matters more is your personality.

A boy may look strong and muscular, but he may not be attractive because he is selfish and thinks too much of himself. A girl may have a pretty face but she may be insensitive and impolite.

What are the qualities that make someone attractive?

1. Being optimistic – having a positive attitude to life and being enthusiastic.
2. Dependability – being reliable and not letting people down.
3. Being a good communicator – sharing their hopes and fears and being a good listener.
4. Showing kindness and consideration for others.
5. Unselfishness.
6. Faithfulness.
7. Moral integrity – having a clear idea of their values and being willing to stand up and be counted if necessary.
8. Confidence – feeling at ease in the company of others.
9. Politeness.
10. Intellectual curiosity – being keen to discover and learn about new things.
11. Respect for others and for the views of others.
12. A sense of humour.

YOUR CHOICE

On your own, study Trinia Newsome's list and pick out the three qualities you think are most influential in making a person attractive. Compare your choices with the choices other people have made.

Sonia's story

When I started going out with Darren, my girlfriends couldn't see what I saw in him. They poked fun at him because of the way he spoke, because of his accent, and because he wears glasses. He's not the most handsome of boys.

But one of the things that attracted me to him was the way he was always polite and helpful, even to strangers. One day at the bus stop there was this woman struggling with her pushchair. None of the other kids did anything, but Darren stepped forward and helped her put it on the bus.

When we went to the fair, Darren was careful to make sure I was strapped in properly when we went on the rides, and we took turns at deciding which rides to go on.

He's a good communicator too. He'll talk to me about anything and he listens carefully to what I've got to say.

DISCUSS

Read Sonia's story. Discuss what she finds attractive about Darren. Is a person's character more important than their looks in making them attractive?

Thomas's Story

I'd always wanted to go out with Terri because she's one of the most good-looking girls in our year, but when I actually went out with her it turned out she wasn't what I expected. All she wanted to talk about was herself and about how boring school was and how she planned to be a celebrity. She was very self-centred and wasn't really interested in what I had to say.

DISCUSS

Read Thomas's story and then discuss the following questions.

1. Why was he attracted to Terri at first?

2. Why did he change his mind about her?

3. What do you think Thomas learned from this experience?

WRITE

'Being unselfish, kind and considerate of other people's feelings are more attractive qualities to have than being clever and good looking.'

Write a paragraph saying why you agree or disagree with this statement.

4.1 Right and wrong

How you behave depends on what your values are.

What are values?

Values are things which you believe in. They help you to determine what you think is right and wrong. They are based on a combination of what you have experienced and what you have been taught by friends, teachers and family. As you grow older, your values may change. Sometimes you will find yourself in a situation that challenges your values.

Jodie, aged 11, has made a list of the things that are most important to her.

Jodie's Top Ten Rules:

1. Don't steal things from other people.

2. Don't be violent.

3. Don't think only about yourself.

4. Don't eat too much junk food or drink too many sugary drinks.

5. Don't stay up too late playing video games.

6. Don't keep quiet when you see something is wrong.

7. Don't interrupt other people when they are talking.

8. Don't litter.

9. Don't hurt animals.

10. Don't disrespect other people.

YOUR CHOICE

Look at the list and decide which points you agree with and why. Give reasons for your views.

Sticking to the positive

When creating rules for yourself, always put things in the positive. If we say to ourselves, 'I must not take things from other people,' all we remember is 'take things from other people'. Therefore, it's really important to keep your thoughts in the positive. For example, 'I must respect other people's belongings'.

WRITE

Look at Jodie's list again. Rewrite her list so that it only includes positive statements.

Then compare your new list with that of another student or pair, to check that they are only positive.

YOUR CHOICE

What other rules would you include? Discuss these in a group, and then write down your rules. Give reasons for your choices, and make sure they're only in the positive.

'It's all changed since great grandad's day...'

Attitudes and values change over time. Your attitudes are likely to be very different from those of your great grandparents, says Sean Lewis.

In the early 20th century, young girls and women who became pregnant were considered to have brought disgrace to their family. The young men who were responsible were expected to marry them. Young women had to live with the shame. Many were sent away to have the child. Some went to mother and baby homes before being forced to give up their babies for adoption. Others risked having back-street abortions.

Homosexuality was a crime and gay people lived in fear of being arrested and imprisoned. The divorce laws were different and it was harder to get a divorce. Many women stayed at home as housewives and the man was the sole breadwinner. Black and ethnic minority people were discriminated against and were the victims of prejudice.

RESEARCH

Many attitudes and values changed in the 1960s. Talk to any of your relatives who lived through the 1960s and/or use the internet to find out about the changes that occurred during that period.

DISCUSS

1. Discuss the changes you found out about in your research.

2. In groups, discuss what you would do in each of the situations below. Do you feel very differently about the different situations? Give reasons for your views.

   a) Your friend wants you to lend them money to buy some cigarettes, despite them having asthma.

   b) You find a £20 note lying on the floor. The next day, someone in your class claims to have lost twenty pounds. However, you suspect your friends may have told them you found a £20 note, so you're not sure whether they're telling the truth.

   c) You're near a fight in the playground. Although you weren't involved, the teacher gives you and everyone involved in the fight a detention.

Different people often view the same situation in different ways. Therefore, while most people would agree that the actions listed below are wrong, they would disagree about which ones are the most or least serious.

YOUR CHOICE

In pairs, rank the following actions in the order of most serious to least serious. Compare your rankings with those of another pair. Give reasons for your decisions.

a) Playing knock and run.

b) Vandalising a car.

c) Stealing a mobile phone for a dare.

d) Riding on a bus or train without a ticket.

e) Swearing.

f) Smoking.

g) Drinking alcohol.

h) Cheating in tests.

i) Cheating in your GCSEs.

j) Bullying someone because they are different to you.

WRITE

1. Pick one of the situations described on these pages. Write a couple of paragraphs about what you would do in that situation, and what you consider to be right or wrong.

2. Imagine you are going to speak in a debate. Pick one of the following statements and list 3–5 reasons to support your argument.

   - 'It is never right to do the wrong thing.'

   - 'It's OK to do a wrong thing, like lying, in order to prevent a greater wrong, like somebody getting hurt.'

RESEARCH

How are a person's values influenced by their religion? Choose two religions, for example Christianity and Islam, and research the values of those religions.

Write a report 3–4 paragraphs long, comparing the religions you have chosen, explaining the values they have in common and those where they differ.

4.2 Who do you admire?

Who you admire depends on what qualities you value.

What is admiration?

We admire someone when we think they are worthy of our respect. People we admire often have a quality or qualities that we like or approve of. Sometimes, we want to be more like that person.

However, sometimes we admire someone we don't really know. We may have formed an opinion of them from what we have seen in the media, for example. Therefore, it is important that even if we admire a quality in a person, we bear in mind that we don't know everything about them.

DISCUSS

Look at the list of people below.

- Which people do you admire?
- Why do you admire them?

Discuss your choices and give reasons for your views.

> The Queen
> Jessica Ennis-Hill
> Harry Kane
> Jeremy Corbyn
> Ariana Grande
> Donald Trump
> Danni and Jack from *Love Island*

Fallen idols — case studies

Tariq, Birmingham

I used to admire Mike Tyson. Tyson was a boxer who became world champion at the age of just 20 in the 1980s. I thought, that could be me. He was strong, driven, and successful at a young age. When I was at primary school, I used to pretend to be Mike Tyson. I would practise my punches and foot moves, and one day I was going to be a great boxer like him.

It was only later on at secondary school that I became aware of Mike Tyson's history. He served three years in jail for rape. Then I read that in 1997, in a boxing match with Evander Holyfield, he bit off part of Holyfield's ear. As soon as I saw those two facts I thought 'That's it.' Tyson is longer a sporting hero for me.

Stacey, Glasgow

I really admired the way Megan from *Love Island* looks. I thought, she's gorgeous. I thought to myself: I can look that good if I try hard enough. But however hard I tried, it was never good enough.

Then I spotted in the papers that Megan had spent over £40,000 on plastic surgery. Her look isn't natural – it's been created. I think this sends out the wrong message to teenagers. Boys expect girls to look like this, and girls can't, because it's so artificial.

I've got nothing against Megan as a person, but I'm no longer going to idolise her or try to look like her.

1. Consider the questions below in relation to the two case studies.

   a) Why do you think Tariq admired Mike Tyson and Stacey admired Megan Barton Hanson?

   b) What made them change their minds?

   c) What do you think their mistake was?

   d) What do you think of Mike Tyson and Megan?

2. In pairs, discuss somebody you have admired. Why did you admire them? Did your opinions change over time? Give reasons for your views.

Think about the person you most admire. Write a short paragraph about what qualities you admire in them, and why.

How the media influence us

The amount a person appears on TV, in newspapers and magazines or on YouTube and social media influences who we admire.

The more media exposure a person gets the more likely we are to admire them. You've probably heard of Jessica Ennis-Hill, who won Olympic gold and silver medals, and Dina Asher-Smith, who is a world-class sprinter. But have you heard of Bethany Firth?

Bethany is a world champion Paralympic swimmer who has been awarded the MBE for services to swimming. But because she has a disability, she doesn't get as much attention.

Do you know any unsung heroes, people who do amazing things that don't appear in the media? For example, you might think of someone who spends all their life looking after someone who was born with learning difficulties or a person who works in a war zone helping refugees. Discuss people who you consider to be unsung heroes.

British values

Some people argue that Britain has a unique set of positive values. These include tolerance, freedom of speech, listening to other people, fair play, justice and equal opportunities. They argue that children should be taught these from a young age at primary school so that we all adhere to them.

Other people argue that these values are not unique to Britain, but are found among many other people in other countries across the world. Rather than teaching British values, we should be taking the best from everywhere, and respecting contributions from the cultures of all different people and countries.

1. In pairs:
   - Do you think there is such a thing as British values? If so, what are they?
   - Compare your list with another pair. Give reasons for your views.

2. In groups:
   - What do you think are particularly good values from other parts of the world? Think about different countries, different cultures, and different religions.
   - Can you learn anything from outside of your own country, culture or religion?

4.3 Regrets and saying sorry

Everyone makes mistakes; what matters is how you deal with them.

Regrets

When we regret something we've done, this means we wish we hadn't done it. Sometimes we act without thinking. Sometimes we rush into things without considering what the consequences will be. At other times we change our mind later and wish we had acted differently.

The important thing to remember is that everyone makes mistakes. It's how we learn. The key thing to do is to reflect on our behaviour and try to change it. This way, we can avoid making the same mistake again in the future.

DISCUSS

Discuss each of the situations below and say what you would do in each case.

- Would it make a difference if you knew the people involved?
- What would you do if the person was your friend?

Imagine you saw someone

- throwing stones at a window
- spraying graffiti on the wall of a bus shelter
- carving their name on a bench in a park.

Would it make a difference if…

- the window was in an empty or derelict building?
- the wall was in a private house?
- the bench was a new one?

Imagine you saw someone

- stealing a bar of chocolate from a shop
- cutting the lock off a bicycle and riding off on it
- climbing up an apple tree to take some apples.

Would it make a difference if…

- the shop was a corner shop or a supermarket?
- you knew who owned the bicycle?
- the tree was in a farmer's field or in a garden?

Imagine you saw someone

- urinating behind a tree in a park
- teasing someone in a wheelchair
- chasing a dog with a stick.

Would it make a difference if…

- they were urinating in a stairway in a block of flats?
- the person had a permanent disability or was temporarily in a wheelchair following an accident?
- the dog had stolen something in its mouth, and did or did not have a collar on?

Are any of the actions listed opposite more serious than others? Write your views on the circumstances in which you think:

a) you should call for help and/or tell an adult

b) you shouldn't do anything.

In groups, imagine you had done each of the things in the list opposite.

- Which ones would you regret?
- Why?
- In what circumstances?

Give reasons for your views.

Saying sorry and making amends

Some people find it easy to say sorry; others find it harder. However, saying sorry is an important way of showing regret and demonstrating to a person that you have learned from a situation. It also shows that you would act differently in the future. There are several rules for saying sorry.

1. You need to genuinely mean that you are sorry. People can tell when you say sorry and you don't really mean it.

2. Avoid saying 'Sorry, but,' as this isn't really an apology. It's a way of saying sorry while also blaming the other person, or excusing your behaviour. A genuine apology has no buts attached to it.

3. Be specific. Say exactly you are sorry for, and why. Explain that you understand why what you did was wrong, and show how you have learned from the experience.

4. Pick the right time. Sometimes it will be too early to say sorry to someone. They may still be angry if you have had an argument, so you need to let them calm down. On the other hand, don't leave it too long. Many couples make sure they say sorry before they go to bed at night, rather than sleeping on a problem, which can make it worse.

5. Don't hold a grudge. Sometimes it is better to apologise and just let things go.

6. Always apologise in person. A genuine apology needs to be done face to face.

What other rules can you think of when saying sorry? Make a list. Try to think of at least three.

5.1 You and your family

Learning how to handle family relationships is an important part of growing up.

There are many different types of family. A lot of families have a mother and a father. Some families have a mother and a stepfather, or a stepmother and a father. Some families have a single parent. Some families have two fathers or two mothers. Some families live in larger extended groups, perhaps with grandparents.

Some people have a carer or guardian and live in care homes or foster families.

Some people have brothers and sisters. Others have stepbrothers and stepsisters and live in what is called a blended family. Others have no siblings at all. Still others may live in larger extended family groups with their cousins.

There is no one type of family. However, your family are the people you spend a lot of time with. As a result, it's important to get on with your family, and the different people within it.

DISCUSS

Read the statements below.

a) 'My mum is the one who gives me the praise, and it's my dad who always tells me off.' Sasha, London.

b) 'I live just with my mum, so she's the one who does everything.' Tom, Leeds.

c) 'I live in a traditional family. My mum does all the cooking and cleaning, and my dad is the one who goes out to work.' Ismil, Birmingham.

d) 'I never argue with my dad, but always argue with my mum.' Cheryl, Newcastle.

e) 'I have a lot more contact with my mum because my dad is always working.' Will, Plymouth

f) 'My mum works, and my dad does all of the housework, and I get to hang out with my dad more.' Sophie, Manchester.

g) 'I have two dads, who both do everything equally with me.' Amy, Portsmouth.

h) 'I have foster-parents who have been really good to me.' Joe, Doncaster.

1. What do you learn from each of them about the type of family the person lives in?

2. What do you learn about the relationships within that family?

Communicating with your family members

In any situation, there will be at least three different points of view. This will include how you saw the situation, how your family member saw the situation, and what actually occurred.

Read Faisal's story.

'My parents wanted me to go to the grammar school, but I didn't. They entered me for the 11 plus exam, which I didn't do any work for, because my heart wasn't in it. All of my mates were going to the local comprehensive. My dad went mental when I failed my 11 plus, and we had a big argument. My mum was much better, and said she thought mistakes had been made on both sides.

When I think back on it, I realise my dad only wanted the best for me, and wanted what he thought would be the best education for me. However, he hadn't communicated that to me. And I realised my mum was right – I'd made a mistake as well. I should have calmly told my parents what I wanted, which was to stay with all my friends from primary school.'

DISCUSS

In groups, discuss what you think were the mistakes made on both sides. What would you have done differently if you were Faisal? How could his parents have handled things differently? Give reasons for your views.

WRITE

Think about a situation where you have had an argument with one or both of your parents or a person in authority. Answer the following questions.

1. Why do you think the argument occurred?

2. Every action is done for a positive reason in a person's head. What positive thing do you think the other person was trying to achieve for you?

3. What were you positively trying to achieve?

4. What do you think really happened?

5. What would you do differently next time?

DISCUSS

Discuss your answers to the writing task with a partner. What can you learn from their experience, and what can they learn from yours? Remember, it is OK to get things wrong occasionally, and to admit that you are wrong in a relationship.

Being positive

For every negative comment we experience, it takes three to five positive comments to counteract it. So, if you want other people to be positive toward you, it is important that you take the lead and be positive towards them.

WRITE

Keep a diary for a week and note down the positive comments you give and receive with a plus (+) and the negative comments you give and receive with a minus (–). Try to give a lot more positive comments than negative comments.

At the end of the week, look at the totals of positive and negative comments. Do you get a lot of positivity from any particular people or activities? You should spend more time with these people or doing these activities. Are there any people or activities that are negative? You should either spend less time with these people or on these activities, or you should talk to these people, positively and constructively, to see if you can change things.

Hugs

Hugs are important, but they need to be long – over 30 seconds long. Scientists have discovered a hug over 30 seconds long releases chemicals into your brain which make you feel good. So if you want to feel better, get a hug from a family member or friend, or ask someone if they'd like a long hug to make them feel better if you see that they are down. Remember respect and consent are important so ask before you give someone a hug.

5.2 What makes a good friend?

How friends treat you is influenced by how you treat them.

There are different levels of friendship. Some people have one close friend to whom they confide everything. Others will have several close friends. Other people will have a large group of friends. Outside of this you might have friends of friends, who you are not so close to but still get on with.

YOUR CHOICE

Read the following statements about what makes a good friend. Which ones do you agree with and which ones do you disagree with? Give reasons for your views.

1. 'A good friend will always keep a secret – unless you have broken the law.' Tim, Cornwall.

2. 'A best friend is a friend for life.' Lisa, Edinburgh

3. 'Friends shouldn't tell tales and try to cause trouble between other friends.' Samira, Cardiff.

4. 'Friends should tell another friend when they have done something wrong.' Toby, Liverpool.

5. 'A friend should stick up for you, especially when you are not around to defend yourself.' Emma, York.

6. 'Friends shouldn't be jealous if you have done better than them at something, but praise you. In the same way, you shouldn't rub it in their face.' Sam, Oxford.

7. 'Friends should tolerate you when you are different, whether it's your face, race, religion or sexuality.' Mohammed, Wolverhampton.

8. 'Friends should share both the good and bad times together.' Nadia, Coventry.

The changing nature of friendships

Friendships can change over time. Sometimes you will become closer to a person. Other times you will drift further apart. This is perfectly natural. Sometimes a friendship may change because you don't see as much of a person, for example when you move to secondary school. You may start spending more time with new friends. You may join a new club, move to a new area, or have somebody else move into your area or join your school. These sorts of changes are normal.

Carla in Year 6

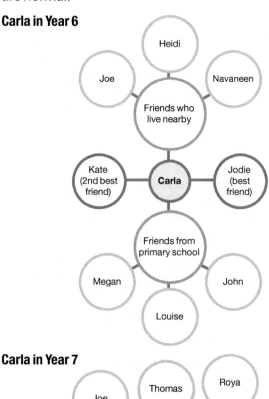

Carla in Year 7

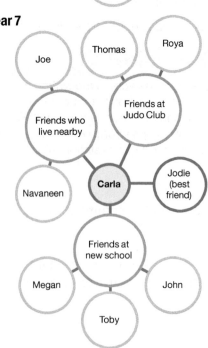

DISCUSS

Study Carla's friendship maps and discuss how they are different.

How should friends behave?

Different groups of friends will have different rules about what is acceptable and what is not acceptable. These rules will depend on who is in the group, what their experiences are, and how they get along with other people in the group.

DISCUSS

Look at the list of rules for Mika's group below.

1. Which rules do you think apply in your group?

2. Which do you disagree with?

Give reasons for your views.

a) Friends shouldn't talk over one another, but respect everyone in the group.

b) Friends shouldn't be negative about people in the group to non-group members, but support them instead.

c) Friends should be there for one another, and be supportive if a member of the group has a problem.

d) Friends should turn up when they have arranged to meet up and keep their commitments.

e) Friends should make time to hang out with each other regularly.

f) Friends should not join opposing groups in sporting events or video game matches.

g) Friends should talk to each other if they have a problem, and avoid going behind each other's backs.

Tolerance

Sometimes people will do something in your friendship group that annoys you. It is important to think about how serious this is. Is it a minor thing that you can tolerate, or ask them not to do again? Or is it a major thing that means you may spend less time with them, or even stop being friends with them? It is also important to recognise whether it is the action and behaviour that you have a problem with, or the person themselves.

DISCUSS

Look at the following list of behaviours.

1. Which ones could you put up with?

2. Which ones would you speak to the friend about, to ask them to change their behaviour?

3. Which ones would mean that you spend less time with a person?

4. Which ones would mean that you could no longer be friends with that person?

a) The friend never makes eye contact and yawns when you are talking.

b) The friend always beats you at video games when you are playing against them.

c) The friend never picks you to be on their team during PE lessons.

d) The friend has decided to go out with your brother or sister, but didn't tell you in advance.

e) The friend stole some money from your parents, and refuses to give it back.

f) The friend has called you a liar and said you broke something at school, even though you know they did it.

g) The friend has started smoking and wants you to try it.

h) The friend is obsessed with sex and talks about it all of the time.

i) The friend spends too much time on their mobile phone using social media.

j) The friend is being horrible to another friend of yours because the other friend is gay.

WRITE

Write your own list of ten rules for friendships.

5.3 Rivalries

Understanding what causes rivalries can help you to deal with them.

Sometimes you may come across a rival. A rival may be a friend or just somebody that you know. The may do similar things to you, so you may find yourself in competition with them.

Some rivalries are just friendly. For example, you may be good at a computer game which your friend is also good at. Such a rivalry can develop into a friendly competition, which is harmless. However, if you or the other person start taking it too seriously, and the rivalry starts producing negative feelings, then it is time to stop and think about the situation.

Susie's problem

I was at primary school and really good at rounders. I really enjoyed playing it as I was the best in my year. So I always got to bat first and always scored well for my team.

When I moved to another school I met this other girl, Kate. She was also good at rounders, and on the first day of PE she was on the other team. We beat her team by one run that I scored at the end.

Since then, it's been like war between us. In PE, we always go on different teams and compete against each other. It's not a nice competition – it can get quite nasty. People on different teams say mean things about us. We've got one mutual friend who's finding it really difficult to be friends with both of us. I've nothing against her really; it's just that we're both good at rounders.

Mike's problem

I used to be really good friends with Conor, until the latest version of Football Manager came out. It started off OK at first – both of us competing online to be the best manager in our league.

We started trading insults as a bit of a joke, but gradually it became serious over time. I don't really care about the game – I just don't want to lose face or the respect of our friends.

DISCUSS

In groups, talk about Susie's and Mike's problems.

1. What do you think the problem is for each of them?

2. How do you think the rivalry can be solved?

3. Have you ever had a rivalry like this which you solved? If so, how did you solve it?

Identity issues

Often when we have a rivalry with somebody it is because they threaten our identity. In Susie's case above, it is about who is best at rounders in the school group. In Mike's case, it is about who is best at the video game in their group of friends. However, both are just games. The games are not really about who Susie and Mike are. They won't care about these games in five years' time.

It is important to remember the following points:

- Your identity doesn't depend on that of the other person – you are independent of them.

- It may be the other person's behaviour and not actually the other person you are objecting to.

- In five years' time, you probably won't even remember the other person, let alone care about the current rivalry. Therefore, it isn't really worth bothering about.

- If you are secure in your identity, you will be immune to any rivalries that develop – you won't care.

- There is always somebody better than you at something, just as there is always somebody worse than you at something.

- Often, the way you communicate with another person in a particular situation reflects the way they will communicate with you.

- If your friends are really your friends, they will support you, whatever happens.

- You are continuing to grow and develop all of your life – things will be very different in a month, a term, a year and 10 years.

DISCUSS

Study the two statements below. Discuss whether you agree or disagree with them and why.

'What's really important is my values and who I am – not whether I am good or the best at a particular sport or activity.'

'How I treat others is the change I can make to a situation if I don't like it.'

Sorting out your emotions

Sometimes with a rivalry you need to work out what is really going on. First, take a couple of minutes to breathe in and out regularly to help you relax and put you into the right state to deal with the problem.

Next, decide who is involved in the rivalry. Is it just you and one other person, or does it involve several people, or groups of people, on both sides?

Think about how the rivalry started. What exactly is the problem? It may be one of a number of things:

- insecurity about identity

- jealousy

- boredom – so people are making the rivalry worse to create a drama

- over-competitiveness

- fear of missing out

- anger about something else.

The last is known as 'misplacement'. This is when we misplace our feelings about one thing onto another. So a person may be having problems at home, but cannot solve them, so they take their feelings out on somebody else by creating a rivalry. The solution to this problem may actually lie at home instead.

DISCUSS

In groups, consider the list of types of problem above.

1. Have you ever experienced one of them directly or seen it indirectly with people you know?

2. How was the problem solved?

3. Make a list of the best ways of solving the types of problem above and give reasons for your views.

4. Compare your list with another group.

RESEARCH

Research a famous rivalry on the internet – it might be between football managers, tennis players, fashion icons, social media influencers (see Unit 10.2) or politicians. What do you think has caused this rivalry? Do you think it's healthy? Do you think this rivalry can be solved?

6.1 Sex: facts and myths

As well as giving pleasure, having sex carries risks. There is the risk of pregnancy, getting an infection or becoming hurt emotionally.

In order to reduce the risks, it is helpful to be aware of some of the myths about how you can get pregnant, to understand what is meant by safer sex and to know what the laws are in the UK about sex.

How much do you know about how people become pregnant?

There are many myths about how to avoid pregnancy.

MYTH 1: *You can't get pregnant if you have sex standing up.*

That's absolute nonsense. Whatever position you have vaginal sex in, standing up or lying down, the girl can get pregnant.

MYTH 2: *You cannot get pregnant if you have only had sex once.*

Again, that's not true. Unless some form of contraception is used, a girl can get pregnant even if she only has sex with a boy once.

MYTH 3: *You can't get pregnant if the boy withdraws his penis before he ejaculates.*

Withdrawal should not be used instead of contraception. Often sperm may leak into the vagina before the boy ejaculates, making it possible for the girl to become pregnant. It's not worth the risk when there are plenty of forms of contraception available (see Unit 6.3).

MYTH 4: *You can't get pregnant if you have sex when you've got your period.*

It is possible to get pregnant during a period, especially if you have a short cycle. Sperm can live in a girl's body for up to seven days.

MYTH 5: *You won't get pregnant if you wash out your vagina immediately after having sex.*

This procedure is called douching. However, it doesn't work to prevent pregnancy.

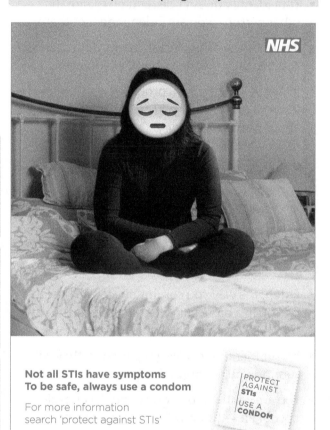

NHS

**Not all STIs have symptoms
To be safe, always use a condom**

For more information
search 'protect against STIs'

PROTECT AGAINST STIs
USE A CONDOM

© Crown copyright 2018 | SH2018-14

So how can you prevent pregnancy? The only *certain* way is to abstain from having sex. However, you can greatly reduce the chances by using some form of contraceptive, though you should be aware that no method of contraception is 100 per cent reliable.

What is safer sex?

There is always some risk in having sex. Vaginal sex carries the risk of pregnancy. Oral and anal sex do not carry the risk of pregnancy but vaginal, oral and anal sex all carry the risk of infection with a sexually transmitted infection (STI). Also, all sexual activity involves emotions of one sort or another and can cause distress if the people involved haven't discussed what the consequences might be.

There is no completely safe way of protecting yourself against catching an STI, which is why people talk of 'safer sex' rather than 'safe sex'. This means using a condom and/or dental dam during sexual activity.

'My boyfriend's attitude is that everything we do, from crossing the road to going rock climbing, is risky, so what's the point of practising safer sex?'

Gina

DISCUSS

1. What would you say to Gina's boyfriend to convince him that he should practise safer sex?

2. What should Gina do if he refuses?

How much do you know about STIs?

STIs can have a range of consequences, from some that are unpleasant to others that are really serious, including life-threatening illness or conditions that can lead to infertility in later life. As with pregnancy, there are many myths about STIs.

MYTH 1: *You can catch genital herpes (cold sores on your penis, scrotum or vagina) from toilet seats.*

This is wrong: you cannot catch an STI from a toilet seat, only from sexual activity with another person.

MYTH 2: *Only people who have sex with a lot of partners are at risk of catching an STI.*

Obviously, the more sexual partners you have, the more at risk you are. You can reduce the risk by only having sex with one partner, but you can't eliminate it entirely.

MYTH 3: *You can always tell if you've got an STI.*

The fact is that it's hard to tell whether you have an STI, because there are often no signs or symptoms. For example, you can have chlamydia without having any symptoms, but if it is not treated it can lead to infertility. The only way you can find out for sure is to get yourself tested at a clinic.

MYTH 4: *You can protect yourself from catching an STI by having a shower before and after having sex.*

This won't protect you against STIs.

Getting treated

You may have heard it said that you needn't worry about having an STI, because it will eventually go away on its own. However, just because there are no symptoms doesn't mean that it's gone away. The only way to get rid of an STI is to have it treated.

Sexual health clinics are easy to access, with some having drop-in clinics, and can provide confidential tests and treatment for STIs.

Note: You will find more details about the different types of STI in *Your Choice Book 2*, Unit 4.

DISCUSS

Identify what you consider to be the three most important facts you have learned from these pages. Then share them in a group discussion.

WRITE

Use the information on these pages to do one or other of the following tasks:

1. Produce a test-yourself quiz consisting of ten statements, some of which are true and some of which are false.

2. Produce a poster titled 'Common Myths about Pregnancy and STIs'.

6.2 Sex and the law

How much do you know about sex and the law?

Fact check

There are a number of laws about sex that are there to protect you.

In the United Kingdom, if you are under 16 you are not legally allowed to take part in sexual activities. (It is unlikely you would be prosecuted for sexual activity with someone your own age, if you were both age 13–16 and had given your consent. However, an adult engaging in sexual activity with someone under 16 would be committing a serious offence.)

Any sexual activity with someone under 13 is illegal.

The age of consent

The age at which you can agree to engage in sexual activities is known as the age of consent. In the United Kingdom, the age is set at 16.

The law is designed to protect people under 16 from exploitation by adults. Anyone having sex with someone aged under 16 can be prosecuted.

The age of consent varies from country to country. In several European countries – Austria, Germany, Portugal and Italy – the age is 14, and it is 15 in France, the Czech Republic and Denmark. In Ireland and some states in the USA the age of consent is 17.

What does consent mean?

It means that you agree willingly to take part in a sexual activity with another person. Both of you must give your consent.

You cannot assume that a person gives their consent. If there are signs that a person is unsure about what you are doing, such as stopping kissing or touching or avoiding physical contact by moving away, you should ask them whether they are happy to continue. If you continue without their permission, you are breaking the law.

The law intends to protect young people against being forced or pressured into having sex rather than to punish teenagers. If you are both 13 to 16 and having sex which you have both agreed to, you are less likely to get into trouble.

Rape and sexual assault

Any sexual activity that is forced upon you, that you are pressurised into doing because you are threatened, or that you did not consent to is against the law. The person doing this to you could be charged with sexual assault, assault by penetration or rape.

It is also illegal for anyone over 18 to encourage you to watch a sex act being performed or to make you watch pornography.

Indecent exposure

It is not an offence to be naked in public in England and Wales. However, if you expose your genitals or pleasure yourself in public so that it causes harm or distress to someone who sees you, then you are committing an offence. This is 'indecent exposure'.

Similarly, it is illegal to have sex in a public place.

Indecent images

It is illegal to share an indecent photo of yourself if you are under 18. This means a photo of you nude, semi-clothed or taking part in a sexual activity. It is also illegal to take a sexual photograph of anyone under the age of 18 and to share it online. Finally, it is illegal to send anyone a text message or email that is threatening or obscene.

Ask Erica

Dear Erica

My boyfriend is 17 and I am 15. We've been going out together for two years and we agreed to have sex. We only did it once, but I'm afraid that if we are found out he'll get into trouble. What does the law say?

Craig

Dear Erica

I am 17. I took a topless selfie and sent it to my boyfriend who is also 17. He shared it with his friends. Did we break the law?

Esme

 **DISCUSS**

Discuss Craig's and Esme's questions to Erica.

Taking 'upskirting' photographs becomes a criminal offence

Taking 'upskirting' and 'downblousing' pictures will land perpetrators in jail and on the sex offenders register.

Under a new law, 'upskirting' is to be made an offence punishable by up to two years in prison.

'If you're a victim then you feel humiliated; this is an invasion of privacy,' said Lucy Frazer MP.

The law is being introduced after predators were seen to target females at festivals and on public transport, with the photos then being shared online.

ROLE PLAY

Someone claims that there's too much fuss made about taking such pictures. They argue that people who take them are only having a laugh. Another person explains to them that it is a very serious matter. Act out the conversation between the two of them, arguing their different points of view.

DISCUSS

Imagine that you are a type of judge known in the UK as a magistrate.

1. Would you give any of these people a prison sentence?

2. Would you let any of them off with a warning?

3. Would you put any of them on probation? (Probation is a period of time where people are monitored on a regular basis. If they break the law again they will receive a tougher sentence.)

4. In addition to the sentence you decide upon, which of the people would you put on the sex offenders register? (The sex offenders register contains the details of people convicted of a sexual offence against children or adults.)

a) A person aged 17 uploads pictures of their former boyfriend/girlfriend in the nude because they are angry with them for breaking off their relationship.

b) A boy aged 14 took an upskirting picture of a member of his class.

c) A person aged 14 is accused of touching someone inappropriately. The offender is deeply ashamed and has written a letter of apology to the person concerned.

d) A man aged 21 admits having sex with a 15 year old but claims he didn't know they were underage.

6.3 Safer sex: contraception

If and when you decide that you are ready to have sex, it is important that you discuss what form of contraception you are going to use. Although most forms of contraception, apart from condoms, are used by the girl, this should be a joint decision and a shared responsibility.

If you are aged 13 to 16, you have the same rights as an adult to obtain free and confidential advice from a doctor, nurse or pharmacist. They will recommend the best method for you and can supply contraceptives without telling your parents.

There are a number of methods you can use. However, to have the best chance of avoiding catching an STI you should use a condom. Some people use a condom in addition to another method of contraception.

Condom facts

The male condom fits over a boy's erect penis. It acts as a barrier, preventing sperm from entering his partner's body when the boy ejaculates.

It is made of latex rubber, synthetic rubber or a very thin plastic. It must be put on before the penis comes into contact with the vagina, anus or mouth, and stay on all the time you are having sex. If it splits, tears or comes off, you must stop and put on another one. If this happens, there may be a risk of pregnancy or a sexually transmitted infection.

Once the couple has finished having sex and there is no longer any contact between them, the condom can be removed. A condom can only be used once. When using a lubricant, remember it must be water-based. Oil-based lubricants can stop a condom working.

Where can you get condoms?

Condoms are available free from some GP surgeries, sexual health clinics, some young people's services and contraception clinics. If you join the C-Card scheme, you will be able to get free condoms from different centres and pharmacies in your local area. You can also buy them from pharmacies, supermarkets, online and from vending machines in some public toilets.

Always buy condoms that have the British Standards Institution kitemark as a guarantee of their quality and do not use a condom if it is past its sell-by date.

The contraceptive pill

This is a very effective method of avoiding an unwanted pregnancy. It is 99 per cent effective if taken properly. However, it does not protect you against STIs. The most common form is known as the combined pill, which consists of two hormones – oestrogen and progestogen – which stop a girl from ovulating.

For the combined pill to be effective, a girl must take one at the same time every day. If she forgets to take a pill, she should take it as soon as she realises, even if that means taking two pills in one day and she will still be protected. However, if she misses two or more pills, the pill won't be effective and you will need to use another type of contraception (e.g. condoms).

Having an upset stomach can stop the pill working effectively. If a girl vomits within two to three hours of taking a pill, her body won't have absorbed it. She should take another pill as soon as possible after the vomiting stops. If it continues for more than 24 hours, she should consult a doctor or nurse.

Is the pill fool-proof?

Provided that you follow the instructions very carefully, the pill is one of the most reliable methods of contraception. However, if you forget to take them or don't stick to the routine as instructed, then you reduce its effectiveness.

There are other very reliable contraceptives available that girls can use, such as injections, implants, coils and patches.

The morning after pill

If a girl feels at risk because she forgot to take her pill, because she had sex without a condom or because a condom split, she can take what is known as the morning after pill to prevent a pregnancy. There are two types – one which must be taken within 72 hours of having had sex and one which must be taken within five days. Whichever pill you take, the sooner you take it the more effective it is likely to be. These pills are available from the doctor, a sexual health clinic or can be bought from a pharmacy.

RESEARCH

On your own, decide which of these statements are true and which are false. If you are unsure of an answer you can search for it on the internet at the Brook or NHS websites.

1. You get more protection if you use two condoms.

2. Condoms are 99 per cent effective if used properly.

3. Condoms don't last forever.

4. You can wash out a condom and use it several times.

5. You can use lubricants like Vaseline® with a condom.

6. Condoms are the only method of contraception that give protection against an STI.

7. Condoms sometimes split.

8. You shouldn't flush condoms down the toilet.

9. Condoms break easily.

10. You don't need to use a condom if your partner is on the pill.

DISCUSS

Compare your answers to the research task in a class discussion.

Ask Erica

Dear Erica
My boyfriend and I got carried away and had unprotected sex on Friday night. I've hardly slept all weekend worrying that I might be pregnant. What can I do?
Alicia

Dear Erica
I'm worried about contraception. My girlfriend says she is on the pill. Is that enough protection if we have sex? Please advise me.
Vikram

WRITE

Compose Erica's replies to the questions above.

RESEARCH

Find out about other methods of contraception, such as contraceptive injections, implants and patches.

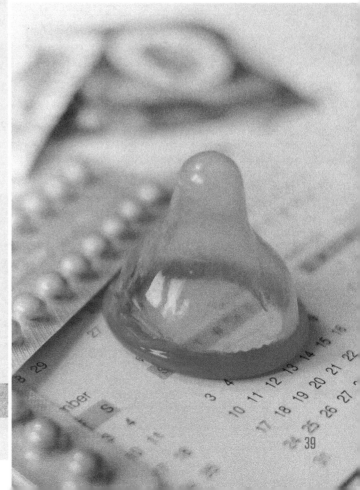

7.1 Exploring your sexuality

The term 'sexuality' refers to your sexual feelings, what you enjoy and who you are attracted to.

What's right for you is right for you

Almost every film, TV programme and book that you come across as you are growing up will probably have some kind of 'love interest' – and it will nearly always be a boy who fancies a girl and/or a girl who fancies a boy. But that's just not how it is for everyone. Some boys fancy boys. Some girls fancy girls. Some boys feel like they ARE girls, and were born in the wrong bodies.

Some girls feel like boys in the wrong bodies. It's complicated! Finally, people fall in love whatever their gender. Fortunately, you live in a time when this is pretty okay. There's far more freedom to be who you are than there was in the past. So whatever your friends tell you, or your parents want from you – or you want for yourself – you'll figure out who you really are.

From *The Girl Guide* by Marawa Ibrahim

DISCUSS

Discuss what Marawa Ibrahim says.

1. What does she say about the different ways people feel about their gender?

2. What does she say about people's sexuality (who they are attracted to)?

3. Do you agree that films, TV and books usually represent boy/girl relationships as the norm?

4. Do you agree that it's easier to be who you want today than it was in the past?

Exploring your feelings

It can be difficult to talk about your sexuality, especially if you are only beginning to explore your feelings. You have the right to keep these thoughts private but when you are ready you may find it helpful to talk things through with someone you trust.

DISCUSS

1. Why might it be more difficult to talk about our sexuality than other parts of our identity?

2. Who do you think would be the best people to talk to about these issues?

Fact Check

Here are some terms used to describe a person's sexuality.

Bi or bisexual: men or women who are attracted to more than one gender

Lesbian: women who are attracted to other women

Gay: men who are attracted to other men; sometimes also used to describe lesbian and gay sexuality in general

Heterosexual/straight: women or men who are attracted to people of a different gender

Sexual orientation: this refers to who you are attracted to and want to have a relationship with

Trans or transgender: people whose gender is not the same as the sex they were given (assigned) at birth

LGBT: lesbian, gay, bi and trans

Like other aspects of our identity, our sexuality can develop and change over time. This is a natural part of growing up. You may have an experience that makes it clear to you what your sexual orientation is, or you may gradually learn how you feel.

Whatever your own sexual orientation, it is vital to accept and respect other people's sexualities. A time which some young people find difficult can be made so much worse by the negative attitudes of others.

Ask Erica

I'm very attracted to this girl in Year 8. I keep fantasising about kissing her. She and I get on really well. I read somewhere that you often get a crush on someone when you're going through puberty. Should I tell her?

Angela

Dear Erica
I heard someone making insulting and abusive remarks about gay people in the playground. I know that's wrong. Should I have done something about it and challenged them or should I have reported them to a teacher?

Dave

Dear Erica
I am so confused! I honestly thought I was gay. I was ready to come out and tell my parents but then Evie started at our school and she is so fit! I found myself flirting with her and she flirted back. I think I want to ask her out but would that be crazy if I am gay? How would I tell her if it didn't work out? I don't know who to talk to about this – I don't know where I belong.

Luke

WRITE

Write your own replies to Angela, Dave and Luke.

DISCUSS

Now look at the responses below and decide whether you agree with the advice.

Dear Angela,
It would be a good idea to get to know this girl better as a friend first. Can you ask her to join in something that you and your friends are doing? You mention it could be a crush. The only way to find out how you feel is to spend time with her. This could also give you an idea of how she might react if you tell her how you feel.
Erica

Hi Dave,
You have recognised that this is hurtful and wrong. Your suggestion of telling a teacher is a good one. They will know what to do next and will take this very seriously.
Erica

Dear Luke,
You are not alone in being confused. Lots of people your age are exploring their sexuality. Relax and don't try to force yourself to decide anything straight away – whether that is being gay, bisexual or something else. Lots of people don't like the idea of labels and there is no need to choose one before you are ready. Get to know a range of people and see what feels comfortable and right for you. If you would like to talk to someone there are agencies that will support you. You could also find out if there is a support group in your school.
Erica

RESEARCH

Stonewall and the Proud Trust are organisations that campaign for and support LGBT communities. Find out from their websites how they can help people of your age, and what youth and support groups are running in your area.

7.2 Sex: your rights and responsibilities

As you learned in Unit 6, when you go through puberty, you become more aware of your sexuality and your sexual feelings. At some point, when you feel time is right for you, you may become sexually active and start to enjoy having sex. You have already learned a lot about the facts and myths around sex, about contraception and about the law. It is also important to know what your rights and responsibilities are.

Consent

It is up to you to decide whether or not to take part in sexual activity with someone. It's your body, not theirs, so it's your choice. You have the right to say no to any sexual activity another person suggests.

It is also your responsibility to make sure that the other person gives their consent willingly before taking part in any sexual activity. If you think the other person is unsure, ask them how they feel and respect what they say. If they say no to what you are suggesting, you must stop. If you persist in asking them to agree, or threaten them in any way, you are harassing them and could land yourself in trouble, as sexual harassment is against the law.

You have the right at any time to say 'stop' if you begin to feel uncomfortable with what you are doing.

It is your responsibility to be aware of the other person's feelings and to stop what you are doing if they ask you to.

DISCUSS

Besides telling you to stop, what other signs can tell you that a person feels uncomfortable with what you are doing?

Talk about what you can tell from someone's body language and how they react to being touched. What can you tell from their facial expressions and whether they maintain eye-contact?

It is your responsibility to pick up on other non-verbal signs and to stop whatever you are doing if you think that's what the other person wants. If you continue, you may hurt the other person emotionally and it may damage your relationship with them. You might also be committing sexual assault.

Your right to protection

You have the right to avoid the risk of pregnancy.

It is your responsibility to discuss what form of contraceptive you are going to use as a couple to avoid an unwanted pregnancy. It should be a joint decision between two people who trust each other.

You have the right to ensure that you are protected from getting an infection when you have sex.

You have the responsibility to agree with the other person how you are going to protect yourselves against getting an STI.

It is your responsibility to get advice from a doctor about methods of contraception that are suitable for you.

It is your responsibility to get yourself tested if you think you have caught an STI and to tell the other person if you have caught an STI, so they can get treatment.

Your right to privacy

You have the right to privacy.

It is your responsibility to keep what you do together between the two of you. You should not go around boasting about what you did together to your friends. It is unfair on the other person. Instead, if you want to discuss privately with a friend what has happened, you can do so. However, you should be respectful and emphasise that what you are saying is private.

You have the right to confidentiality when seeing a doctor or nurse.

Your right to express your feelings

You have the right to a full and frank discussion with the other person about everything connected with having sex.

It is your responsibility to make sure that you communicate how you feel and what you will and will not allow by setting boundaries. You also need to understand the other person's feelings by listening to what they have to say and agreeing boundaries.

Your right to choose

You have the right to love and be attracted to whoever you want, whatever their gender. It is common to have a crush on someone of the same gender when you are going through puberty.

It is your responsibility to accept that people may be attracted to people of the same or different genders and choose their partners accordingly.

DISCUSS

Discuss the situations below. What are the rights and responsibilities of the people involved?

1. Scarlet told Liam she didn't like the way he was kissing her, but he went on doing it till she pushed him away.

2. Theo keeps touching Becca's knee and pushing up against her. When she complains, he says she's just playing hard to get.

3. Rachel confided to Jasmine that she was going on the pill and swore her to secrecy, but Jasmine told the rest of their friends.

4. Jed allowed Jenny to take some revealing pictures of him when they were a couple. But they've had a row and broken up and Jenny's posted them online.

5. Jacob has had sex with two girls and thinks he has caught an STI.

6. Sinead has announced she's bisexual. Her friends won't stop teasing her about it.

WRITE

Share the key points you have learned from thinking about these rights and responsibilities. Now write a statement saying what the most important points are.

7.3 Attitudes to sex

Attitudes to sex vary from person to person and from generation to generation.

How you feel about sex

Not everyone feels the same way about sex. Some people feel ready to have sex sooner than others, who may choose not to have sex until they are older. You should decide for yourself what you want to do and not feel under pressure to have sex until the time feels right for you. Neither should you feel ashamed if you feel ready to have sex before some of your friends do.

Sex can happen between two people who don't have a long-term relationship and do not expect that having sex will to lead to a committed relationship. It can occur between two people who are friends or two people who have only just met.

There can be some risks involved. For example, couples who have just met may be more likely to have unprotected sex, increasing the risk of an unwanted pregnancy or of catching an STI. Also, as the two people involved may not know each other well, they may have different expectations of what it happening.

Fact check

According to Public Health England, a young person is diagnosed with a sexually transmitted infection every four minutes.

A survey of young people by Public Health England revealed just under half of the people surveyed had not used a condom when first having sex with a new partner.

DISCUSS

Discuss the information in the Fact check. Are you surprised by these facts?

Ask Erica

Dear Erica

I was at this party and I could see that this boy fancied me and I fancied him. My friends said they had to go, but I decided to stay on. I'd had a few drinks, so when the boy took my hand and said he had something to show me, I went upstairs with him. We went into one of the bedrooms and when he started kissing me, I kissed him back. I wanted to tell him to stop, but I got carried away and we had sex. When we'd finished, he said he'd got to go and just left. I feel ashamed. I don't want ever to put myself in that situation again.

Sam

WRITE

Write Erica's reply in which she reassures Sam and offers advice on how to avoid or prepare for a similar situation should it occur in the future.

DISCUSS

In groups, discuss these opinions:

1. 'Sex with someone you've just met is fine, so long as both parties give their consent.'

2. 'Sex with a long-term partner feels better because you really love each other.'

3. 'Casual sex can be a problem, because one person may think it will lead to something more, like a relationship.'

4. 'You shouldn't have sex until you are older and until you are sure that you're in love with someone.'

5. 'It's more acceptable for boys to sleep around than girls.'

6. 'Sex with a long-term partner is much safer. They respect you more as a person.'

7. 'If both people know what they're doing, casual sex can be fun and enjoyable.'

8. 'If I'd been more choosy about who I slept with, I wouldn't have ended up pregnant, not being absolutely sure who the father was.'

9. 'As long as they're not breaking the law, people should be able to have sex whenever they feel ready and not be judged for it.'

Fact check

Attitudes to sex vary from country to country. Religion can be an important factor influencing people's attitudes.

For example, premarital sex, masturbation and oral sex may be seen as unacceptable in some cultures.

Attitudes alter from generation to generation.

Nicola Wordsmith explains the effect this has on teenagers and their parents.

Sex used to be a taboo subject. Seventy years ago, adults did not talk about it openly. Rather than discuss the facts of life with their children, many of them avoided having a discussion with their children by giving them a book to read or ignoring the subject and hoping that one of their peers would enlighten them.

Today it's different. Attitudes have changed. Sex is no longer a taboo subject. Today's teenagers and their parents can talk openly about sex.

DISCUSS

Discuss whether you agree that today's teenagers can talk to their parents openly about sex. Do you feel comfortable talking to your parents about sex?

Ask Erica

Dear Erica

My parents keep trying to talk to me about sex. They tell me things I'd rather not hear and keep asking me questions I'd rather not answer. How can I make them realise I find it really embarrassing?

Carrie

Dear Erica

My parents started off talking to me about sex in general terms, which was fine, but now that I've got a girlfriend I don't want to talk to them about what we do together. I shouldn't have to, should I?

Carl

WRITE

Write Erica's replies to these two people.

8.1 What is bullying?

Bullying takes many forms – all of them hurtful.

Bullying includes:

- Physical bullying – pushing or hitting someone, threatening them if they won't hand over money or belongings, stealing from them or damaging their things.

- Verbal bullying – calling someone names, making hurtful remarks, spreading rumours.

- Sexual bullying – putting pressure on someone to do something they don't want to do, stalking or harassing them.

- Emotional bullying – ignoring or deliberately leaving someone out, constantly making them feel that they are worthless and criticising everything they do.

- Racial bullying – picking on someone because of the colour of their skin, their race, religion or country of origin; making fun of the way they speak and the way they dress.

- Cyberbullying – posting nasty comments about someone on social media.

For details of cyberbullying and how to deal with it, see Unit 9.2.

Who gets bullied?

People get bullied for lots of different reasons. Often, it's because they are different in some way. They may dress differently, for example they may cover their heads with a scarf. They may like the 'wrong' music. They may come from a different part of town. However, it is important to remember that no one deserves to be bullied.

DISCUSS

1. Discuss the different types of bullying.

    a) Are some forms of bullying more hurtful than others?

    b) Which kind of bullying might take longer to detect?

2. Study Kyle's and Martin's comments. What do they tell you about bullying and how other people may allow the bullying to continue because they do not intervene?

'I was picked on because I'm overweight. They called me names and made fun of me in games lessons. What upset me most, and disappointed me, was that my best friend didn't do or say anything.'

Kyle

'There was this boy in our class who would fly into a rage if people made fun of him. Some of the class thought it was funny and would deliberately provoke him. We just let it happen until one day he picked up this model that one of the bullies had been making and smashed it to pieces. He got blamed and shortly after transferred to another school.'

Martin

How does it feel to be bullied?

Bullies often say that they are just having a laugh. But it's not very funny if you are on the receiving end. Bullying hurts.

'I thought all the world was against me. I thought it must be something I'd done. I went to see the counsellor. He made me realise that it wasn't my fault. It's stopped now, but it's taken me a long time to start feeling good about myself again.'

Jay

'Every time I went out they'd shout at me and say disgusting things about me and my family. It got so bad that I stopped going out. I stayed in my room and cried a lot. Or I'd shut myself in the bathroom. I kept it all bottled up inside.'

Sammie

'It went on for a year. They would empty my books out of my bag, and once they poured glue into the bag. They found my homework and said they'd tear it up if I didn't let them copy it. They threw my PE kit in the showers. They made me so miserable that I started truanting. I was scared to tell anyone because they threatened to beat me up.'

Imran

'They just ignored me. It was as if I wasn't there. Even Tanya who used to be my best friend told me to get lost when I tried to talk to her. When they started to spread rumours about me, I'd had enough. So I finally talked to my mum and asked her if I could change schools.'

Orla

DISCUSS

Read the statements from the four children and talk about what it feels like to be bullied.

DISCUSS

Read the poem 'And how was school today?', then discuss these statements and say why you agree or disagree with them.

1. The person in the poem is too frightened to tell anyone about what is happening.

2. They do not understand why they are being ignored.

3. Their parents have no idea that they are being bullied.

4. The person in the poem is a girl.

5. The way that they are being treated at school makes them very unhappy.

6. The person in the poem hides their feelings.

7. They go to their bedroom to avoid being seen to be upset.

8. This is a very sad poem.

9. The poem makes me understand what it is like to be bullied.

And How Was School Today?

Each day they ask: And how was school today?
Behind my mask, I shrug and say OK.
Upstairs, alone, I blink away the tears
Hearing again their scornful jeers and sneers.
Hearing again them call me by those names
As they refused to let me join their games.
Feeling again them mock me with their glares
As they pushed past me rushing down the stairs.
What have I done? Why won't they let me in?
Why do they snigger? What's behind that grin?
Each day they ask: And how was school today?
Behind my mask, I shrug and say OK.

By John Foster

8.2 Dealing with bullies

What's the best way to deal with bullies?

YOUR CHOICE

Here are statements about how to deal with bullies. Which ones do you think are good ideas and which do you think are bad ideas? Give your reasons.

1. The best thing to do is to run away.

2. Keep calm. Look the bully in the eyes and tell them to leave you alone.

3. Walk away, and at the first opportunity tell an adult.

4. Threaten them that if they hurt you, your older sibling or cousin will beat them up.

5. Fight back. It will make them stop bullying you.

6. Whatever you do, don't get drawn into a fight. Fighting is only likely to aggravate the situation and get you into trouble.

7. Call them names and spread rumours about them to make them understand what it feels like to be bullied.

8. Ignore it. Make out that it doesn't hurt you. Bullies thrive on weakness.

9. There's not much you can do. You just have to put up with it until eventually they pick on someone else.

10. Don't get upset and don't cry in front of them.

Why do some people become bullies?

Some people bully because they think it is fun to tease other people and to upset them by threatening them. It makes the bully feel powerful.

Other bullies are driven by jealousy. They may pick on someone whose family is better off than their own, or someone who is clever.

Some people bully because they are prejudiced. They bully people whose cultures are different from their own. Such bullying is racist.

Many bullies are unhappy and insecure. They bully as a way of making up for what they see as their own inadequacies. They may turn to bullying to make up for their own lack of achievement. Making people frightened of them is a way of giving themselves some status.

Others are bullied themselves at home, so they grow up believing that taking it out on someone who is weaker than them is the way to look after themselves.

There is evidence that children who are victims of bullying at school have a higher than average chance of becoming bullies themselves.

DISCUSS

Discuss the reasons why people become bullies. Can you suggest any other reasons?

WRITE

You find out your friend is bullying someone. What could you say to them about their behaviour? Write a paragraph.

ROLE PLAY

One of you finds out that your friend is bullying someone. Act out a scene in which you talk to the bully about their behaviour.

DISCUSS

Read the poem 'If you want to join the gang'. Then discuss the questions below, giving reasons for your views.

1. What do you think of the poem?

2. Is it acceptable to stand by when such bullying is occurring?

3. What could the person in the poem have done instead?

If you want to join the gang

They said that I had to do it,
If I wanted to join the gang.
So I waited with them outside the school
When they picked on Tony Chang.

I was there when they jumped on him,
I was there when they ripped his shirt.
I was there when they emptied out his bag,
And kicked his books in the dirt.

They said that I had to do it,
If I wanted to join the gang.
But now I feel bad that I was there.
When they picked on Tony Chang.

By John Foster

How to beat the bullies

- Tell an adult. It is important to speak out. Bullies are afraid you'll speak out, because they know they are in the wrong.

- Try to take no notice. Try not to let them see how upset you are. Bullies like to upset people. But if they get no response, they may leave you alone.

- Get your friends to stick up for you. The more of you who stand up to them, the less they can get their own way.

- Don't change your behaviour. Trying to please bullies will not make any difference.

- Act quickly. The longer you let the bully get away with it, the worse it will become. Often, the bullying will begin with some teasing or name-calling before it escalates into threats, intimidation and violence. Once the bully realises that you are not going to tell an adult they are in a position of power over you. They know that they can step up their bullying without having to worry about an adult interfering.

Remember: Telling an adult about bullying is not telling tales. Bullies have no right to upset you. You have a right to feel safe and happy.

Ask Erica

Dear Erica
This older boy has started picking on me. He comes and finds me at breaktimes. He and his mates take my bag and throw it around so I can't reach it.

They've started to ask me for money. I gave them a pound, but now they are asking for more. What should do?

Amir

WRITE

Draft Erica's reply to Amir.

ROLE PLAY

Act out a TV discussion in which a panel of people with different experiences of bullying discuss the best ways of dealing with different types of bullying.

Take on the following roles:

a) someone who has bullied others

b) someone who has been bullied

c) someone who was a bystander.

9.1 Personal safety online

The internet has many benefits, but needs to be used with care.

Is the internet good or bad?

By Erica Stewart

Even those who stress the dangers of the internet admit that it has had a beneficial effect on our lives. In particular, it has greatly improved the way we communicate with each other. It's now possible to communicate instantly with people on the other side of the world, which wasn't possible in the past and you can keep in touch with family and friends when you are away from home.

The internet has made it possible to find information quickly and easily. You can use it to learn about any topic. If you want to buy something you can research the product, then buy it online.

The internet provides entertainment too. There are computer games you can play, or you can watch amusing videos that people have posted on YouTube.

But there are drawbacks. Anyone can post what they want on the internet. If they don't like you, they can bully you by posting messages that are hurtful and say things that are untrue. The internet can give you false or biased information. You need to be certain that any information you use comes from a site you can trust.

Another danger is that you can become addicted to the internet and spend all your time chatting to your friends or playing computer games, instead of meeting your friends in real life, or getting exercise by playing outdoors.

There's also the problem of hackers stealing information about you and the risk of not knowing who you are actually talking to in a chatroom. There's the danger that they could be a sexual predator.

And there's the fact that pornography is readily accessible.

So the internet has considerable drawbacks and needs to be used with care. But do the bad points outweigh the good points? I'm not sure that they do.

DISCUSS

What bothers you most about the internet? Think about Erica's article, then read the statements below and discuss each concern. Which views do you share? Is there anything else that worries you?

1. I was horrified when a picture of a naked woman suddenly popped up while my 10-year-old brother was playing a game on the computer.

2. I'm concerned about the violence in the games my brother plays.

3. I think my sister is addicted to the games she plays. She won't even stop to eat.

4. I'm worried about fake news and the way the internet can be used to spread lies and rumours.

5. What concerns me is that you can't be certain that a person you chat to is who they say they are.

6. What bothers me is the way bullies can use the internet.

7. I'm concerned that my brother watches porn.

8. It upsets me when people post unkind comments about my friends, or post photos that make them look silly.

Pornography

Pornography is sexually explicit pictures or videos of naked or semi-naked people having sex or who look as if they are having sex. The pictures aim to excite the people who see them.

Pornography does not present a realistic picture of sexuality and relationships. It shows sex without any emotional involvement.

It can affect people's attitudes towards sex by:

- giving a distorted view of sex in which relationships do not matter

- implying that mutual consent isn't necessary before having sex

- suggesting that practising safer sex isn't important

- presenting violent sex as normal

- presenting women as sex objects and ignoring women's pleasure

- making it seem as though loving relationships aren't important.

DISCUSS

'Pornographic sites should be more difficult to access. You shouldn't be able to access them simply by pretending you are over 18.'

'Parents should block you from accessing pornography.'

Discuss these views.

Darcia's story

I was 14 when I saw an ad in the paper for teenage models. I've always wanted to be a model so I booked an appointment. When I got there, the photographer explained that I would be modelling swimsuits.

I was quite excited. But as the shoot went on, he asked me to reveal more and more of myself. That's when I became uncomfortable and said no. He got angry, at which point I decided to leave.

When I spoke to another girl who had stayed at the shoot, I realised the whole thing was a scam. The photographer had asked for £60 to help build up a portfolio of photos for her. She never saw a portfolio – he was just after nude pictures of young girls he could sell illegally on the internet.

He's been reported to the police. I hope they catch him.

DISCUSS

1. What do you think of Darcia's story?

2. What could she have done differently?

Give reasons for your views.

YOUR CHOICE

In pairs, decide which of these statements you agree with and which you disagree with. Give reasons for your views.

Compare your decisions with another pair. Were they the same or different?

1. 'I was on the bus, and a young lad sat down next to me and started watching porn on his mobile phone. This is completely unacceptable.'

2. 'Feminism says women should be allowed to do what they like with their bodies, so if they want to earn some more money online providing glamour shots and videos, why should we stop them?'

3. 'Anything that results in a woman being seen as a sex object should be banned.'

4. 'We're never going to be able to completely police the internet, so it's better that we regulate pornography, rather than making the entire industry illegal and driving it underground.'

5. 'Pornography ruins sex for both men and women, as it creates unrealistic body images and expectations.'

6. 'There should be stronger age controls on pornography on the web, and internet providers should be made responsible for restricting access to pornography.'

9.2 Cyberbullying

Cyberbullying is a particularly nasty form of bullying.

Using the internet to bully other people is called cyberbullying. It can take various forms:

- sending offensive emails or texts
- posting insults or lies about someone on social networking sites
- putting embarrassing photos or videos online.

Typical types of cyberbullying are name-calling and spreading false rumours about someone.

The main reason children say they are cyberbullied is because of their looks. Children can also be picked on because of their ethnicity, religion or sexuality.

Trolls

A troll is someone who uses social media platforms to send messages that are deliberately hurtful, offensive and inappropriate. Trolls wait for a response and then post more unpleasant comments in order to provoke a reaction.

Trolls hide behind their screens and use fake names to remain anonymous. They often pick on people who are vulnerable, such as someone with a disability, or they harass their victim because of the person's ethnicity, religion or gender.

Fact check

Trolls are guilty of a crime and can be sent to prison or fined.

In 2011, Sean Duffy, a 25-year-old man, was sentenced to 18 weeks in prison for posting a comment on the tribute page of two teenagers who had died, poking fun at them.

Top tips to deal with trolls

- However much you want to respond to their lies and cruel comments about you, don't do so. Replying will show them that they have upset you, which is what they are trying to do.

- Report them to the moderator of the site on which the message was sent. The providers of platforms such as Twitter and Facebook have a legal and moral duty to protect you.

- Block the trolls from contacting you.

- When you receive any message that is hurtful, your first reaction may be to delete it. Whatever you do, don't keep on reading it, or you're likely to get more and more upset. But don't delete it. Save it or screenshot it. You may need it as evidence of how the troll is trying to get at you.

- Don't suffer in silence. Tell an adult you can trust.

- Don't try to sort it out alone. Sharing what's happening will help you to work out a strategy for dealing with it.

- Never forward hurtful or embarrassing messages or photos of someone else. Delete them or report them to an adult you trust.

- Inform the school, even if it's taking place outside school. They may be able to help.

- Contact the police and show them the copies of the messages that you have kept.

- Encourage anyone else you know who has been targeted to speak out and report it.

DISCUSS

In groups, discuss these views and say why you agree or disagree with them.

- 'Trolls are basically cowards who hide their identity by sending anonymous messages.'

- 'Trolling is not free speech, it's hate speech.'

- 'There should be tougher sentences for people convicted of trolling.'

- 'Trolling is just people having a laugh. I don't know why there's such a fuss about it. People should be more thick-skinned.'

- 'The social media companies should do more to shut down the accounts of trolls.'

- 'The government should introduce tougher laws and harsher sentences for trolling.'

- 'The police should spend more time investigating such crimes and bringing perpetrators to justice.'

- 'Individual citizens should report all instances of trolling immediately.'

Be streetwise

Think carefully about what you do in public. Someone may have a smartphone and could take a picture or video of you and share it on the internet without your permission.

Don't reveal your location. There are many websites and apps that share your location including Facebook. It is unwise to share your location, especially on websites that anyone can access. Check that your privacy settings on your phone and computer keep your locations private.

Don't be afraid to admit you made a mistake. The online bully may be a stranger who you have allowed to friend you online, so you are afraid what your parents will say if you tell them. But which is worse: allowing the abuse to go on and letting the bully get away with it, or admitting what you've done? You may be embarrassed by what the bully has posted about you, but it's far better to tell your parents than to allow it to continue. We all make mistakes. Do what's right and block and report them, whatever they've threatened to do. And if you can't tell your parents, tell another adult you trust.

Ask Erica

Dear Erica
My friend is very upset because someone has been spreading rumours about her online and she's worried that people will think they are true. How can she get them deleted?

Karen

WRITE

Draft Erica's reply.

9.3 Protecting your identity online

When you are online, you need to take care not to reveal too much personal information.

Think carefully about what you put online. You never know who can access the material, or whether the material has truly been deleted or removed or is still out there somewhere. You don't know who the information, pictures or images are being shared with.

Your profile online (on a game site, on social media or anywhere else where you may spend time) needs careful thought. You might want to use it to define your online self, but be really careful about giving out too much personal information (where you live, where you go to school, where you hang out).

There are a few reasons why this is a bad idea. First and foremost, no matter how careful you are, you really don't know who could be reading it. You might be on a safe site where it is mates only, but you are still not completely in control of who can read what you post. Friends have friends, who have friends... The information in your profile could be used by a stranger pretending to be someone they think you'll like and trust, or it could be used to work out where you live.

Always take care when giving out personal information such as your name, your address or your school. Even if you are chatting to someone you know, you don't know who else could be checking it out – the internet is a public place!

It's also a good idea not to use a picture of yourself as your profile pic – make it your pet, your favourite band or search out an image that you think is a great reflection of who you are.

Be aware when you're posting pictures of yourself. Say you've been playing around with make-up and you've taken a selfie where you think you look fab (and a lot older than you are). Would you want a stranger to see that version of you? Equally, that film of you and your best mate re-enacting your favourite videos? That will be there forever, which is a loooong time.

So think about what you're posting. Not only the funny/weird pictures – we've all posted some of those – but comments too. Think back three years—the clothes you liked wearing, the books you read, the music you loved – are you into the same stuff now? I doubt it

Whatever you're raving about online now will be searchable forever…Think before hitting 'send'.

From *The Girls' Guide to Growing Up Great* by Sophie Elkan

DISCUSS

Discuss the advice given in the text extract. What do you think are the most important points the author makes?

Unwanted emails

Beware of emails from people you don't know. Everyone gets emails that randomly appear in their inbox. Often they are just junk mail or spam. Whatever you do, don't let curiosity get the better of you. They could be from someone who wants to trick you into giving them your email address. Do not reply! And never ever be tempted to open an attachment or click on a link. Not only could it contain an unpleasant message or image, but it could contain a virus or malware, giving someone else access to your computer or phone.

Be careful about who you let join your contact list in a chatroom. If it's someone you don't know or are unsure about, then block them. The same applies if someone starts sending you hurtful messages online. You don't have to read them!

Ask Erica

Dear Erica

I'm really worried that this person I was chatting to online has managed to track down where I go to school and where I live. What should I do?

Alfie

Dear Erica

I opened this email that appeared in my Inbox that said I'd won a prize and all I had to do to claim it was to send them my name and address. I told my friend and she said not to because it was a scam. It said the prize was worth £50 and I want to claim it. What should I do?

Leila

Dear Erica

I was chatting to friends using Snapchat. There was an option where the photo only appears for 10 seconds, and then the photo disappears. So I took an embarrassing photo of myself, not wearing very much! However, I've learned that a friend managed to take a screenshot of it, and is now sharing the photo with people I don't know. What should I do?

Heidi

WRITE

Compose Erica's replies to Alfie, Leila and Heidi.

WRITE

Imagine that you have been asked by a campaign group THINK BEFORE U CLICK to give them details of what advice they should offer. Make a list of your top five tips.

RESEARCH

Find out what advice is available in leaflets and on websites about staying safe online. What organisations or campaigns can you find that give advice about online safety?

10.1 State management

Every day we make decisions. Some of the decisions will be good, but some of the decisions could be better. Before we start to make decisions, we need to be in the right mental, emotional and physical state to make them. That means we need to manage the sort of state we are in.

The best way to manage the state we are in is to connect all of the parts of our body that help us to think – our head, our heart and our stomach. The best way to do this is through balanced breathing – your teacher will provide you with information on this.

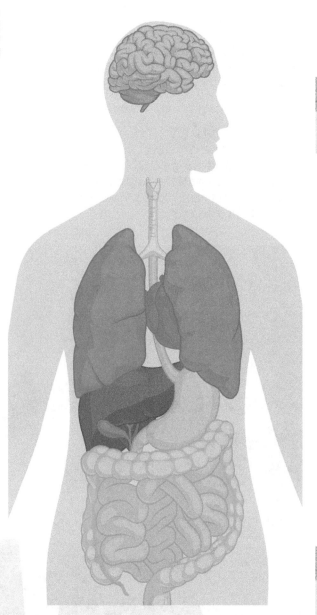

1. Focusing on your head

The 'head brain' is responsible for how we perceive the world. It processes the information from what we see and hear. If someone says something like, 'I can't get my head round that', they are using their head brain.

The highest function of the head brain is creativity, which includes thinking about different things in different ways.

DISCUSS

In groups, think about how you make good decisions. What helps you? What hinders you?

2. Focusing on your gut

If you've ever felt 'butterflies in your stomach' when you've been nervous or 'gone with your gut' to make a decision, this is because you've been getting signals from your 'gut brain'. This consists of two thin layers of nerve cells that go all the way from our lips and mouths through to our stomach, our intestines and our bottoms.

Scientists call this 'brain' the enteric nervous system (ENS). It is responsible for self-preservation – our very survival. This means that the gut brain is very good at prompting us to take action. It is responsible for deciding whether we run or fight in a stressful situation. It is also where we find our core identity.

If someone says something like 'Let me digest that', 'That was a gutsy move', or 'I can't swallow that', they may be talking about their gut brain.

The highest function of the gut brain is courage.

DISCUSS

Think of situations in which you relied on your gut instinct to determine how you reacted to the situation, for example, times when you have felt threatened. Share your experiences in a group discussion.

3. Focusing on your heart

This is where most decision making should start, focusing on our emotions, including our desires and our values. The heart sends messages to the head brain about how we feel.

If someone says something like 'I feel heartbroken', or 'My heart isn't in it', or talks about someone being soft or hard hearted, they may be talking about their heart brain.

The highest function of the heart brain is compassion.

DISCUSS

Think of a situation where you were compassionate to somebody, or they were compassionate to you.

1. How did it make you feel?

2. How can you be more compassionate in your life?

3. In pairs, talk about making a good decision. Notice the language the other person is using. Are they thinking with their head, gut or heart?

Making good decisions

First, make sure you have completed a balanced breathing exercise.

Think about the decision you want to make, such as what you want to do this evening. Continuing with balanced breathing, bring your attention to your heart. Feel why you want to make the decision, and what desire is behind this decision. Think about what connections you want to make to other people and feel the emotions connected to this decision.

Move your attention to your head. Think about the different outcomes for this particular decision. Consider how creative you can be with this decision – are there any other options? How do you see and hear yourself making this decision? What are the consequences and outcomes for this decision?

Move your attention back to your heart. Check if the heart is happy and aligned with what the head is saying.

Then move your attention down to your gut. Digest the implications of this decision. Does it fit with your core identity and preserve and add to who you are? What action do you need to take on this decision?

Move your attention back to your heart. Check that the heart is happy and aligned with what the gut is saying.

Now you are ready to make your decision, be creative with it and take action.

DISCUSS

1. In pairs, think about a decision you have to make, such as what you want to do at the weekend.

2. Note what you desire, how you perceive it, what you think about it and what action you are considering.

3. Then do the exercise above.

4. Finally, discuss with your partner what you now desire, how you now perceive the decision, what you now think about it and what action you are now taking. Talk about any differences and notice the language you are using.

In groups:

5. Talk about a good decision you made. Why was it a good decision, and were all three brains involved?

6. Then talk about a bad decision you made. Why was it a bad decision, and what did you ignore from one or more of your brains? What would you do differently in the future?

   Give reasons for your views.

RESEARCH

The idea of the 'brains' in our gut and heart is new. See what else you can find out about these ideas by researching online.

10.2 What influences your decisions?

Something that influences you has some sort of effect on you and your decision making. Sometimes we are very aware of things that influence us – such as our friends telling us what is trendy or new, or our parents telling us not to do something. Sometimes influences can be more subtle. For example, you may see a new item of clothing mentioned on the internet. Then it's mentioned on a fashion show on TV, and in several fashion magazines. Then there are more adverts for it on TV, and then suddenly it's everywhere, and you want to buy it.

YOUR CHOICE

In pairs, look at the following list of things that influence you. Rank them in order of which you think has the most impact on your life, and which has the least. Then compare your answers with another pair. Give reasons for your views.

a) Parents

b) Siblings

c) Grandparents

d) Extended family such as cousins

e) Close friends

f) Classmates at school

g) The internet

h) Facebook, Twitter, Instagram or other social media sites

i) Local newspaper

j) National newspaper

k) Magazines

l) Celebrities

DISCUSS

Sometimes we can be influenced to do a good thing and sometimes to do a bad thing. Look at John's story. What should John have done instead?

John's story

We were at a sweet shop. My friend dared me to steal a chocolate bar. I wasn't hungry, but I did it anyway, because I wanted to show off to my friend.

As we were leaving, the shop owner challenged me, and made me reveal the chocolate bar. My friend ran for it and got away, leaving me in trouble. The shop owner called my parents. I will never forget the look of disappointment on my mum's face, and my dad shaking his head. I was lucky – the shop owner didn't call the police. I could have got a criminal record for what I did. I should have listened to my gut – I knew what I was doing was wrong.

Media influencers

The media also shapes our values by manipulating us through influencers. Influencers do a new type of job which has appeared in the last 10 years.

Social media influencers have large numbers of followers on one or more social media platforms, such as Facebook, Instagram, Twitter and/or their own website. They make money by selling advertising space alongside their online content, which is then viewed by hundreds of thousands, if not millions of people.

Lele Pons is one such influencer, based in the USA. She has over 22 million followers on Instagram, and 8 million subscribers on YouTube. She is also a brand ambassador for CoverGirl, and works as an actress.

DISCUSS

In groups, look at the following statements about social media influencers. Which ones do you agree with? Give reasons for your views.

1. 'I like social media influencers, especially the ones who tell me what video games are coming out, and which ones are cool and the best to play.' Tom, Oxford

2. 'Social media influencers are a waste of time. They're no substitute for real-life recommendations.' Kelly, Manchester.

3. 'I like looking at what fashion they're wearing, but apart from that, they're harmless.' Jess, Carlisle.

4. 'They're just out there to sell things and make money from the people sponsoring them.' Toni, Bristol.

5. 'They're really good, especially for fashion tips and where the best bargains are.' Jodie, York

6. 'Like everything, it's OK in moderation. I might check out what they're doing once a week, but that's it.' Adele, London.

Opportunity cost

Opportunity cost is a term that comes from the subject of economics. The opportunity cost of something is the next best alternative that exists, which you've lost because you've done something else. Opportunity costs are caused by us having unlimited wants, but there only being a limited amount of time, money and things.

Imagine you want to buy a snack. You have £2. You could spend the money on an ice cream with a flake. Or you could spend the money on a can of drink and a small bar of chocolate. If you decide to buy the ice cream, the can of drink and bar of chocolate are the opportunity cost of buying the ice cream.

Alternatively, you might be thinking about what to do one evening. You could go out with your friends to the cinema. Or you could stay at home and do your homework and then watch some TV. If you stay at home and do the homework and then watch TV, the opportunity cost of this is the trip to the cinema with your friends.

DISCUSS

In pairs:

1. Think about what you did last weekend, and what you could have done instead. What was the opportunity cost of what you did last weekend?

2. Now think about this weekend, and the different opportunity costs that exist. Does this change what you are going to do this weekend? If so, how could you use your time more valuably? Give reasons for your views.

WRITE

Keep a diary of what you do for a week, and the opportunity costs involved. Then use your diary to plan the following week. Do you plan to make any changes?

11.1 Smoking facts

The real costs of smoking are high.

Fact check

One cigarette contains 4,800 chemicals, 69 of which are known to cause cancer.

Smoking-related diseases cause 100,000 deaths a year in the UK, and worldwide smoking is the cause of 6 million deaths.

Half of the teenagers who currently smoke will die from smoking-related diseases.

Smoking damages your health

When you smoke you breathe in several poisonous substances – carbon monoxide, tar and various irritants. In addition to being the cause of 90 per cent of deaths from lung cancer, smoking has been linked to other cancers, such as cancer of the mouth and larynx.

Smoking is also the cause of chronic lung diseases such as bronchitis and emphysema. Smokers are twice as likely to die from coronary heart disease as non-smokers.

Smoking is addictive

Two-thirds of smokers would like to give up smoking. But people find it hard to quit because the nicotine in tobacco is addictive. Smokers suffer withdrawal symptoms if they stop smoking, becoming anxious and craving a cigarette.

Smoking is expensive

A packet of cigarettes costs, on average, £10.40 in 2018. A person who smoked 20 cigarettes a day would spend £3,796 a year on cigarettes.

Smoking is dirty

Smoking is dirty and smelly. Your breath smells of smoke and it can make your hair and clothes smell too. Heavy smokers can get yellow teeth and nicotine-stained fingers and nails.

Why do people start smoking?

Everyone knows that smoking is bad for you, says Erica Stewart, yet still there are some young people who take up smoking.

Why do they start? There are a number of different reasons, but one of the most common is that their friends smoke. Charlotte is 17 and started to smoke when she was 12. 'All my friends smoked and I didn't want to be left out of the group.'

Jem, 16, said that he started because both his parents smoked. 'I grew up with smokers, so it was accepted as normal behaviour in my family.'

Misha, 18, said, 'I thought it looked cool and I wanted to appear grown up. Before I realised it, I was hooked.'

Cora, 16, said, 'I was curious. I just wanted to see what it was like.'

Smoking causes mouth and throat cancer
Get help to stop smoking at www.nhs.uk/quit
Sterling
Superkings Green
20 Cigarettes
Smoking kills – quit now

DISCUSS

Discuss what the teenagers say about why they started smoking. What do you think are the main reasons why people start to smoke?

1. In pairs, act out a scene in which one of you tries to persuade the other, a friend who has just started to smoke, to give up.

2. As a group, act out a scene in which a group of smokers put pressure on someone to start smoking.

Write a list of 'Ten things you should know before you start smoking'.

Smoking myths

MYTH 1: *Occasional smoking is harmless.*

Every cigarette you smoke affects your health. People who only smoke a few cigarettes a week or at social gatherings are putting themselves at risk.

MYTH 2: *It's OK to smoke occasionally when you're pregnant.*

Smoking can damage unborn babies. Anyone who thinks they might be pregnant should give up smoking immediately.

MYTH 3: *Non-smokers who complain about smoke-filled rooms are just killjoys.*

Being in a room where lots of people are smoking means that you are inhaling the dangerous chemicals that are in cigarette smoke. Non-smokers who live with smokers are at risk of developing smoking-related diseases.

Passive smoking

Passive smoking is when smoke from other people's cigarettes harms somebody who is not smoking. This has been medically proven, and is the reason why smoking is banned in public places, including schools and hospitals, and even in private taxis. However, adults are still free to smoke at home, even though they may be harming their children's health.

Look at the following statements. Decide which ones you agree with and why.

1. 'It would be good to ban smoking in homes where there are children, but it would be impossible to enforce.'

2. 'Passive smoking never did anyone any harm. My dad smoked in our house, and I turned out all right.'

3. 'You can tell the kids who have a parent who smokes – their clothes smell of cigarettes.'

4. 'People have died from passive smoking, from lung cancer. It ought to be taken much more seriously.'

5. 'Typical government – sticking their noses in where it isn't wanted. We eat fatty foods and drink too much, as well as smoking. It's our choice if we want to do something that's bad for us.'

Smoking during pregnancy

Smoking can do real harm to an unborn baby. This is because the baby suffers from a lack of oxygen when the mother smokes. Also, the chemicals in cigarettes are easily passed from the mother to the unborn baby. Babies born to smokers tend to be smaller in size, and are at greater risk of birth defects.

Imagine you know an expectant mother who is smoking while pregnant.

- How would you persuade her to stop smoking?

- What difficulties do you think you might have when persuading her?

In pairs, one of you take the role of the mother and the other the person trying to persuade her to stop smoking. Act out the conversation.

Stopping smoking has many immediate health benefits. It can increase your lung capacity and improve your blood circulation, giving you more energy, boost your immune system, improve your fertility and reduce your stress levels.

Visit the NHS website to find out what support is available to those who wish to quit smoking.

11.2 Smoking versus vaping

Is vaping safer than smoking?

What are e-cigarettes?

Electronic cigarettes, unlike traditional cigarettes, do not contain tobacco. Instead they contain liquid nicotine. There is a mechanism which heats the nicotine and turns it into a vapour which smokers inhale and exhale. This is known as vaping.

Because they do not contain tobacco, e-cigarettes do not contain tar and the other harmful chemicals found in tobacco. But they do provide the nicotine that is addictive. If you smoke an e-cigarette you also breathe in a mixture of chemicals, such as those used to flavour them and chemicals produced during the heating and vaporising process.

What are juuls?

A juul is a type of vaporiser that looks like a USB stick. Juuling as a form of vaping has become very popular in America. Juuls come in a variety of flavours, such as crème brulée and mango. They leave a fresh scent which is far more pleasant than the strong smell that comes from burning tobacco when you smoke.

However, while juuling and other forms of vaping avoid the harm that inhaling tobacco smoke causes, they are by no means completely safe. Research suggests that e-cigarettes are less harmful than cigarettes, but that they can damage a person's health by leading to nicotine addiction. Until recently nicotine has been regarded as addictive rather than carcinogenic, but researchers have found that it causes changes in cells that could be a precursor to cancer.

DISCUSS

Say why you agree or disagree with these views.

1. 'Until they are proved to be safe, the sale of juuls should be banned.'
2. 'Vaping is one big science experiment. There is no knowing what the long-term effects might be.'
3. 'It's better to vape than to go on smoking.'

Kicking the habit

More and more people are giving up smoking, says Amy Jackson.

According to figures released by Public Health England in 2018, the number of smokers is declining. Every year 400,000 successfully give up smoking. It is estimated that the smoking rates among adults is set to fall from its 2018 level of around 15 per cent to around 10 per cent by 2023.

Fewer women smoke than men. While 17 per cent of men are smokers, the percentage for women is 13.3.

Sixty per cent of smokers would like to quit. The number of people in Britain who were using e-cigarettes in 2018 was 3.2 million.

DISCUSS

1. In groups, discuss which of the following statements you agree with. Give reasons for your views.

   a) 'The problem with vaping is that it's targeted at young people. Look at all the lovely different flavours that are advertised.'

   b) 'Vaping is less harmful than smoking, so it must be a good thing.'

   c) 'Vaping is like smoking. Some companies are trying to make it cool just to make money.'

   d) 'Vaping tastes great, much better than cigarettes, without the harmful side effects.'

2. A smoker who wants to quit asks you for advice on the pros and cons of vaping. In pairs, discuss what you would say to them.

Fact check

- It is illegal to sell tobacco to anyone under 18.
- All forms of tobacco advertising are banned.
- Cigarette packets must carry a government health warning.
- Smoking is banned in all enclosed public places and workplaces.
- Displays of tobacco products are not allowed in large shops and stores.
- Smoking is banned in cars carrying children.

ASH (Action on Smoking and Health)

ASH campaigns for laws to be introduced with regard to smoking. These include:

- setting a minimum price for tobacco
- an annual increase in the price of tobacco of 5 per cent above the rate of inflation
- a total ban on smoking in cars
- a ban on smoking outdoors
- a ban on actors smoking in theatrical performances
- a warning to be given if there is smoking in a film.

DISCUSS

Work in pairs to discuss one of the following:

1. How effective is the ban on selling cigarettes to anyone below the age of 18? Should shopkeepers who sell cigarettes to under 18s be banned from selling cigarettes?

2. Should there be a total ban on smoking in cars?

3. Smokers argue that they have the right to smoke. Should there be separate rooms in workplaces where people can smoke?

4. Non-smokers argue that they shouldn't have to breathe in smoke produced by smokers. Should smoking be banned outdoors?

5. Do you think putting up the price of cigarettes by increasing the tax on them is the best way of getting people to stop smoking?

Now come together as a class to share your conclusions and the reasons for them.

12.1 What are drugs?

Any substance that alters the way your mind or body works is a drug.

Medicinal drugs

Drugs are important in the treatment of many illnesses. As well as helping to cure infections, drugs are also used to prevent diseases. You can be inoculated, for example, against measles and tetanus. This medical use of drugs has helped to eliminate diseases such as diphtheria and polio.

Drugs are also used as painkillers. You can buy some painkillers like paracetamol at chemists because they are considered safe to use if you follow the instructions, though they can be dangerous if you take too much. Other painkillers like morphine are extremely powerful and can be addictive, so their medical use is strictly controlled.

Social drugs

Some drugs are accepted by society and are not illegal. The most common is caffeine, which is found in tea, coffee, chocolate and high-energy drinks. It is a mild stimulant, but you should not have too much of it. That's why supermarkets are being asked to control sales of high-energy drinks to young people and not sell them to under-18s.

The other socially acceptable drugs are nicotine and alcohol, both of which are dangerous. Nicotine is highly addictive and is found in tobacco, which contains tar and various chemicals known to cause lung cancer and other lung and heart conditions. *(For details of the effects of smoking and vaping see Unit 11.)*

Alcohol is dangerous when consumed to excess. It can cause unconsciousness and even death and can damage your liver. It can lead to addiction and alcoholism and ruin people's lives. *(For more about the effects of alcohol and the laws about alcohol see Unit 8 in Your Choice Book 2.)*

Illegal drugs

Some drugs are illegal for you to possess or to sell because they are considered to be dangerous and likely to damage your health. They include MDMA (ecstasy), cannabis, ketamine, heroin and cocaine.

The law divides illegal drugs into three classes according to how dangerous they are considered to be. Class A are those that are considered the most dangerous and Class C the least dangerous.

Although they are illegal and you risk harming yourself by taking them, lots of young people ignore the risks and take them anyway.

DISCUSS

1. Study the article above. In groups, discuss how society regards some drugs as acceptable while others are illegal.

   a) If alcohol and tobacco had just been discovered would they have been made illegal?

   b) Which class, if any, would you put them in?

2. 'If people want to take drugs they should be allowed to. It's their body and if they want to risk taking drugs they shouldn't be prevented from doing so. Making drugs illegal benefits only the criminals who manufacture them and the dealers who supply them.'

   Discuss this view, saying why you agree or disagree with it.

Why do young, people start taking drugs? Luke Haines investigates.

The teenagers I spoke to gave a variety of reasons.

'I didn't have the confidence to say no,' says Lucy, who began to take MDMA when she was 14. 'My best friend said she was going to try some and I was afraid of what she'd think if I didn't try it.'

Megan said she had a similar experience. 'My friends put pressure on me. I didn't want to feel left out.'

A number of teenagers said that they took drugs because it gave them a thrill. 'It's exciting,' said Blair. 'You know it's risky and it's something adults disapprove of.' His friend Tristan agreed, 'It's a way of rebelling isn't it? Of letting adults know they can't control you.'

'If I'm honest,' says Liam, 'I got into drug taking because I wanted to appear grown up.'

Another reason is curiosity. 'I'd heard so much about how you felt if you took drugs. It sounded exciting,' said Jem. 'I was curious to find out what it was like.'

'I wanted to escape from all the problems I was having at school and at home,' said Joel. 'Getting high was my way of trying to shut them out.'

Several of the teenagers said boredom was the reason. 'I was bored,' said Ben. 'There's nothing else to do round here.' Toni agreed, 'If there was more to do, there'd be less reason to do drugs.'

DISCUSS

In groups, list the reasons the teenagers give for starting to take drugs.

1. What do you think is the main reason teenagers start taking drugs?

2. Put the reasons in order, starting with the main reason, then compare your views in a class discussion.

What should she do? Sally's story

My brother Dave is two years older than me. He'll be 16 next year. We got along all right until about six months ago, when he started going about with this group of older boys. On Saturday he was out with his new mates. I wouldn't normally have gone into his room, but Mum asked me if he had any dirty washing. So I went in. It was a right tip. Dave never puts anything away. Which is why I opened the drawer to put some clean clothes away and saw the envelope.

Inside were some pills. I don't know what they were exactly. But I knew that they were drugs. At first, I didn't know what to do. I'm still not sure that I'm doing the right thing. Dave will probably never forgive me. But tonight when Mum and Dad come home from work, I'm going to tell them.

DISCUSS

Is Sally doing the right thing? What would you do if you were Sally?

ROLE PLAY

What do you think Sally's parents will say to Dave? In groups of three, role play the scene in which they speak to him.

RESEARCH

Find out more about the medicinal use of drugs, including antibiotics and painkillers.

12.2 What effects do drugs have?

People who take recreational drugs, such as MDMA and amphetamines, say they do so to help them have a good time when they are out with their friends. Some drugs help them to relax, others create a feeling of extreme happiness. But regular drug use can affect your whole life.

Your health

Regular drug-takers often lose weight. They pick up infections easily and get sores on their bodies. If they inject drugs they may get hepatitis or HIV.

If you take a drug regularly, your body may get used to it, so that you have to take larger and larger doses for it to have the same effect. This is known as tolerance.

Your body can become so dependent on having the drug that you become addicted to it and cannot do without it. Many drugs are addictive. Once addicted, if you stop taking these drugs you may suffer from withdrawal symptoms.

Your relationships

Drugs can affect your relationships with your family and friends. Drug-takers often try to hide the fact that they take drugs. They become moody and depressed. Their relationships with their partner, friends and family may break down completely.

Your work

Drug-takers often lose interest in everything. Their schoolwork suffers and they get poorer marks. They start to truant because all they want to do is spend time with other drug-takers.

Crime

Drug-takers need cash to buy their drugs from dealers. Dealers lure young people into working for them in return for free drugs. Others start to steal from their family and they may turn to crime to feed their habit.

Different drugs have different effects, as shown in the table.

Type of drug	Effect on the body	Examples
Stimulant	Speeds up the rate at which messages are sent to and from the brain, making you feel more confident and alert.	caffeine, nicotine, amphetamines, MDMA (ecstasy), cocaine
Hallucinogen	Heightens your senses, so that you may see, hear, touch, taste and smell things that are not real, or have a distorted perception of things that are real.	LSD, ketamine, magic mushrooms, cannabis
Painkiller	Blocks nerve impulses.	aspirin, heroin, ketamine
Depressant	Slows down the rate at which messages are sent to and from the brain. Makes a person more relaxed and uninhibited. Affects your concentration and co-ordination.	alcohol, cannabis, heroin, morphine, codeine, solvents, temazepam
Performance enhancer	Improves muscle development.	anabolic steroids

In groups, discuss which drugs you think are the most dangerous. Give reasons for your views.

How drugs affect individuals differently

There are a number of factors that influence how a drug affects someone: the drug, the individual and the environment in which the drug is used.

The drug

The effect depends on the type of drug, its quantity and quality. Obviously, the greater the amount used, the greater the effect. Similarly, how the drug affects you will be influenced by its purity.

The individual

Everyone is different. The same amount of a drug from the same batch can affect two individuals in totally different ways. For instance, your body size and how fit you are can cause your reaction to the drug to be different. Another factor is whether you have taken the drug before and developed a tolerance to it.

The environment

Where and when you take the drug are important factors, such as whether you are alone at home or with a group of friends at a party, and what sort of mood you are in. Also, if you have been drinking alcohol it can influence how a drug affects you.

Discuss and make a list of ten things that can go wrong if you take illegal drugs.

To use or not to use — it's your choice

Teenagers explain why they've chosen not to take drugs.

‘My aunt's a heroin addict. I've seen how drugs can ruin a person's life. I'd never be tempted to use them.’

‘I saw this film about a girl who died from taking ecstasy. I'm not prepared to take the risk.’

‘It would wreck my chances of succeeding as an athlete. My coach has warned me how stupid I'd be to take anything and given me a list of banned substances.’

‘My parents have talked to me about the risks and they'd be horrified if I took drugs. I don't want to let them down.’

‘My ambition is to travel and I wouldn't be able to go everywhere I wanted if I got caught with drugs.’

What do you think are the best reasons for not taking drugs? Discuss this in groups and give reasons for your views.

Act out a series of interviews for a TV programme *Teenagers Talking* in which a number of teenagers give their views on drugs and drug taking. Decide who is going to be pro drugs, who is going to be anti-drugs, and who is going to be somewhere in between.

1. What are anabolic steroids?

2. Why do athletes take them?

3. What are the risks of taking them?

Use the internet to research these questions and produce a PowerPoint® presentation giving the answers.

13.1 Healthy eating

Eating well helps to keep you fit and healthy.

What is a healthy diet?

A healthy diet is a balanced diet that provides all the nutrients that your body needs, as shown in the diagram.

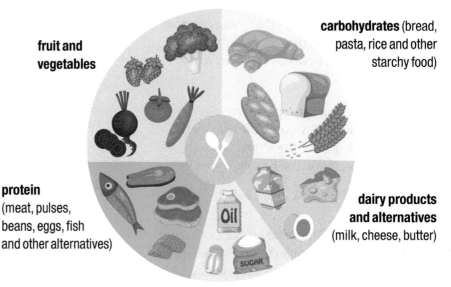

fruit and vegetables

carbohydrates (bread, pasta, rice and other starchy food)

dairy products and alternatives (milk, cheese, butter)

fats (butter, oils)

protein (meat, pulses, beans, eggs, fish and other alternatives)

A healthy diet is also a diet that contains the right amount of food. If you eat too much you can become overweight. If you do not eat enough of the right foods, you can become ill.

Eating a diet high in fruit, vegetables and fibre can reduce the risk of cancer and heart disease. Obesity is the second biggest preventable cause of cancer, after smoking.

Fact check

There are more overweight children in London than in any other major city in the world.

A recent survey of 1,400 children aged 7–12 found that one in three ate unhealthy foods, such as chocolate, crisps and takeaways, more than three times a week.

More than 50 per cent didn't have a single portion of vegetables every day.

Forty-four per cent did not have any fruit each day.

Nearly a quarter had sweets or chocolate every day.

What are Junk Foods?

Certain foods are called junk foods because they are high in calories but low in nutrients. Junk foods may contain lots of saturated fat, added sugar and/or added salt. Junk foods include, crisps, chocolate, sweets, cakes and biscuits.

If you eat a healthy diet, you can treat yourself to junk foods every now and then. But if you eat junk foods too often, you will not get all the nutrients you need for a balanced diet and you are likely to become overweight.

Junk foods are also bad for your teeth because they contain so much added sugar or salt. Pieces of food stick to your teeth and create acid which causes decay and cavities.

Soft drinks contain sugar which damages the enamel that protects your teeth.

WRITE

Produce a script or a comic strip in which a character called Edna Eatwell tries to convince another character, called Steven Snackalot, why he should stop eating junk foods and eat a healthy diet.

Top tips for healthy eating

1. Eat a variety of foods. This will give you all the nutrients that your body needs.

2. Eat plenty of vegetables and fruit. You should have at least five portions a day.

3. Eat fish twice a week. One of these should be oily fish, such as salmon, tuna or mackerel. These fish contain omega 3, which helps to keep your heart healthy.

4. If you are vegetarian, you will need to eat other foods that contain omega 3, such as walnuts, tofu and rapeseed oil. Vegetarians and vegans need to make sure that they are still getting all the nutrients they need. Make sure you are eating foods rich in iron, calcium and vitamin D, which are essential for bone growth during your teenage years.

5. Avoid snacks that are full of salt like crisps and biscuits. Don't sprinkle lots of salt on your food. Ready meals, processed meat such as ham or sausages, soups and pasta sauces also contain a lot of salt.

6. Avoid snacks that contain lots of sugar. You need no more than seven teaspoons of sugar a day. One 330 ml can of fizzy drink contains nine teaspoons of sugar. The more sugar you have, the more likely you are to put on weight.

7. Cut down on saturated fats which can lead to a build-up of cholesterol and damage your heart.

8. Drink plenty of water. You need between 1.2 and 1.5 litres of water daily to replace the water you lose. You can get this by drinking low-fat milk and sugar-free drinks and drinking tea and coffee in addition to water.

9. Eat three meals a day. If you eat regularly you are less likely to feel hungry in between and to snack on unhealthy foods.

10. Don't miss breakfast. A well-balanced breakfast gives you the energy you need for the day. Eat plain breakfast cereals rather than sugar-coated ones and have brown-bread toast spread with margarine rather than white-bread toast spread with butter.

DISCUSS

Discuss the reasons for each of the ten top eating tips.

WRITE

Produce a storyboard for a TV advert aimed at people of your age on how to eat healthily.

What's in your lunch box?

Martin: A jam sandwich, a packet of crisps, a carton of orange juice and a bar of chocolate.

Tula: A brown bread roll with cheese, a packet of nuts, a pot of yoghurt and a bottle of water.

Max: A sausage roll, a piece of shortbread, a banana, a candy bar and a can of cola.

Sasha: An egg sandwich, a piece of fruit cake, an apple and a can of lemonade.

DISCUSS

1. Which of the four children has most healthy lunch? Give the children marks out of 10 for their lunches. Explain the reasons for your scores.

2. How could the children with the lowest scores change the contents of their lunch boxes to make them healthier?

WRITE

Produce a leaflet for parents offering advice on what to put in a 12-year-old's lunchbox.

RESEARCH

Some people are vegetarians. Others are vegans. What is the difference? Find out what they will and will not eat. Research why people decide to become vegetarians and vegans.

Some people will not eat certain foods for religious reasons or will only eat foods prepared in a particular way. Research Jewish and Islamic food customs.

13.2 You and your weight

Whether you put on weight depends not only on the foods you eat and how much you eat, but also on the rate your body uses up the calories in your food. This is called your metabolic rate. Different people have different metabolic rates. If you have a slow metabolic rate, you use up the energy in your foods more slowly than someone with a faster metabolic rate and are more likely to put on weight.

A healthy weight

With the media often promoting the 'thin' body ideal, it may be difficult to know what a healthy weight is and how it can be achieved. The internet may be full of ideas for miracle diets, but people come in all different shapes and sizes: if you eat a healthy, varied diet and take part in physical activity, your weight should stay healthy. […]

Being overweight

Being overweight or obese can affect your self-esteem and increase the risk of a number of health conditions, including type 2 diabetes and heart disease. If you are overweight, eating a healthy, varied diet and maintaining an active lifestyle can help you to lose weight. This will also help you feel better, as you are giving your body all the nutrients, vitamins and minerals it needs.

Fad diets

If you are worried about your weight, don't be tempted to follow one of the popular 'fad' or 'crash' diet (diets that seriously limit the amount of food you can eat or ban food groups from your diet completely). These might lead to weight loss in the short term, but these diets are very difficult to maintain and as soon as you start eating normally again you are likely to put some, if not all, the weight back on. They can also make you feel unwell as they can leave the body lacking in energy and a number of important nutrients. These diets can have other unpleasant side effects, for example cutting out carbohydrates leaves you feeling tired and irritable, suffering from headaches, nausea, dehydration and dizziness – hardly a quick fix to feeling great about yourself!

Skipping meals, especially breakfast, doesn't help either as this can leave you feeling so hungry that all you can think about is food. Eating breakfast has also been linked to a lower risk of gaining weight.

Eating a varied diet and keeping active will help you to maintain a healthy weight and a healthy attitude towards food!

(British Nutrition Foundation)

DISCUSS

In groups, discuss the advice given in the article. What do you think are the three most important points the author makes?

WRITE

A friend of yours is thinking of going on a crash diet. Write them an email or a letter explaining why you don't think it's a good idea and trying to persuade them to see a doctor before they start.

Should junk food advertising be banned?

The mayor of London plans to introduce a ban on all adverts for junk foods on buses, tubes and trains.

MPs are so concerned about the effects on your health of eating too many junk foods that they have come up with these five suggestions:

1. Introduce tougher rules on adverts for junk foods and ban any adverts before 9pm.

2. Ban shops from putting sweets, chocolate and other unhealthy foods at the ends of food aisles and beside checkouts.

3. Ban the use of branded characters, for example from TV programmes and films, to promote unhealthy foods.

4. Limit price promotions, such as 'buy one, get one free', and reduced price offers on unhealthy food and drinks.

5. Introduce labelling giving the calorie content of meals in restaurants and cafes to encourage healthier choices.

The Irish government is banning vending machines in all schools.

The sugar tax – will it work?

In 2018 the government introduced a tax on sugar in soft drinks. The amount of tax a company producing fizzy drinks has to pay depends on the amount of sugar in the drink.

To cut down on the tax they have to pay, companies such as Fanta, Ribena and Lucozade have reduced the amount of sugar in their drinks. But other companies may simply raise the price of their drinks.

When a similar tax was introduced in Mexico in 2014, it led to a 12 per cent drop in the number of fizzy drinks consumed in a year. But will the UK's sugar tax achieve what it aims to do and lead to a reduction in the number of people who are overweight?

DISCUSS

1. Discuss what the sugar tax is. Do you think it will be effective? Give your reasons.

2. Do you think the sugar tax should be extended to other foods that contain lots of sugar, such as sweets, cakes and biscuits?

3. Should the UK government ban vending machines in all schools, as the Irish government has done?

4. Discuss the views below in groups, then share your opinions in a class discussion.

   a) 'It's not up to the government to tell us what to eat. We should be able to eat what we like. It's our choice.'

   b) 'It's right that the government should be concerned about junk foods and should encourage us to eat healthily.'

   c) 'What the MPs suggest won't change people's eating habits.'

RESEARCH

What restrictions are there on advertising junk foods? Are there any plans to introduce tougher rules?

14.1 Exercise

Exercise benefits both your mental and physical health.

Why exercise is good for you

Stuart Lewis explains why exercise keeps you fit and healthy.

Exercise is good for your whole body and for your mental health.

- When you exercise, your body produces chemicals that make you feel good.
- Exercising helps you to sleep better.
- Exercise can help you when you are feeling low and depressed.
- Exercise helps you to have a positive outlook on life.
- Exercise can give you a sense of achievement.

Exercise is good for your appearance and can make you look better.

- Exercise burns up the calories in your diet.
- It can keep your weight down or help you to lose weight if you are overweight.
- Exercise keeps your muscles toned.
- Exercise can help to stop you getting ill.
- Exercise keeps your heart healthy and helps to prevent heart diseases.
- Exercising will keep your bones strong.

ROLE PLAY

'Exercise is boring. I don't do any except in games lessons at school.'

'I don't have time for exercise. I'm too busy playing computer games or watching videos.'

'Why should I bother about exercising? I get fed up with people telling me how to spend my time.'

Discuss what you would say to these three people to try to convince them that exercise is important. Then, with a partner, role-play a scene in which one of you tries to persuade the other to start exercising.

The three elements of fitness

Stamina

Exercise increases your stamina or staying power – your ability to keep going without getting out of breath. It helps to keep your lungs in good condition. When you exercise you breathe more quickly and deeply because you need more energy and use up more oxygen.

The kind of exercise that stimulates your heart and lungs is known as aerobic exercise. It includes activities such as walking, jogging, running, cycling and swimming, as well as games like football, netball and basketball.

Strength

Exercise builds up your muscles and makes you stronger. You don't have to lift weights. There are exercises you can do at home without needing any special equipment, such as press-ups, burpees and step-ups.

Suppleness

Exercise develops your suppleness. If you are supple, you are more flexible. You can bend and stretch your body more easily and you are less likely to injure yourself. There are stretching exercises you can do at home to improve your suppleness.

Exercise: your questions answered

Q. *Will exercise help me to grow more quickly?*

A. I'm afraid not. Your growth rate is determined by when you go through puberty, not by the amount of exercise you do. So exercise will develop your muscles, but it won't make you taller.

Q. *Can I take anything to increase the benefits of exercise?*

A. Don't start taking any substances that people claim will increase your performance, except anything your doctor prescribes, such as for asthma. And whatever you do, don't take steroids.

Q. *Why are steroids dangerous?*

A. Anabolic steroids are a manufactured version of the male hormone testosterone. They are taken by bodybuilders to build up their muscles and used by some athletes to try to improve their performance. However, they have a lot of side effects. For example, women who take them can develop facial and body hair and become more masculine. They can affect a teenager's growth.

RESEARCH

Find out more on the effects of taking anabolic steroids and why they are banned in all sports.

An exercise challenge

If you find it hard to motivate yourself to take exercise, set yourself an exercise challenge.

It could be to:

- run for 10 minutes without getting out of breath
- walk 5 kilometres
- swim 30 lengths of the swimming pool
- cycle round the playing field 20 times
- play a tennis match lasting half an hour.

DISCUSS

In groups, discuss how much you think a person should exercise each week. What are the benefits? Are there any drawbacks? Give reasons for your views.

Addicted to exercise?

Dan is from Newcastle and this is his story.

I started running when I was 12. Gradually, I got really into it. I was running an hour a day, then two hours every day, then running morning and evening. The more I ran, the better I felt inside. I kept pushing myself to run faster and faster and faster.

But gradually I noticed I had fewer friends. They complained I was busy all the time – that running was taking over my life. I wouldn't see anyone on the weekend, I would be running instead.

When I wasn't invited to my best friend's birthday party, I was really upset. She said to me, 'There's no point, you'll be out running.' That's when I realised things had got out of control.

I still run every day, but only for an hour. Now I make sure that I spend time with my friends as well and I do other sports, like football at least once every two weeks. Running is good, but it shouldn't take over your life.

DISCUSS

1. In pairs, discuss why you think Dan became addicted to exercise.

   a) At what point do you think Dan should have realised what was going on?

   b) What advice would you give to somebody like Dan?

2. Doctors recommend half an hour's exercise every day, to help you live longer. Imagine you know someone who doesn't exercise at all, or someone who does more than 20 hours exercise each week.

   a) What do you think the advantages and disadvantages are for each of these people?

   b) What advice would you give them?

14.2 Exercise, sleep and your mental health

Exercising regularly will improve your fitness, your mood and your sleep.

Exercise keeps our heart, body and minds healthy healthy. There is evidence that exercise can help in depression, anxiety and even protect you from stress.

Most of us feel good when we are active. So – don't worry about not doing enough – get started by building a bit more physical activity into your daily life now. Even a small change can make your heart healthier and make you feel happier.

Why does exercise make me feel better?

When you exercise it releases 'feel good' chemicals called endorphins in our brain. It also affects chemicals called 'dopamine' and 'serotonin' which are related to depression and anxiety.

Exercise can help brain cells to grow. In your body, regular exercise makes your heart, muscles and bones stronger and work better.

Activity can help you feel more in control, which helps when you are worried or stressed. You can even make new friends and have fun when you exercise with other people.

How much activity is enough for me?

Any activity is good. You should try to do some activity every day. Regular exercise for about 40 minutes which gets you out of breath, five times a week, will have the best results on your body and mood.

Sarah's Story

'It's been a tough time. We had family problems and then I had exams on top.

I started to get really stressed out, couldn't relax or concentrate at school. Sometimes I found myself just bursting into tears.

I've been talking to a counsellor and starting running helped me to get some space for myself.

I've really improved in how far I can go, but mostly I run because I enjoy it. It's given me my energy back.

My sleep has got better and I don't feel so depressed any more. A friend has asked if she can run with me sometimes. I'm kind of ready for that now.'

from 'Exercise and mental health: for young people', a factsheet produced by the Royal College of Psychiatrists

DISCUSS

1. How did taking up running help Sarah overcome her stress?

2. What do you learn from the article about how exercise is good for your mental health?

Fact check

Not sleeping enough contributes to an increase in fat because sleep regulates the hormones directly linked to appetite, willpower and mood.

Teenagers need between 8 and 10 hours' sleep per night.

As you go through puberty, you need a good night's sleep to help you grow. Sleep is as important as healthy eating and exercise to keeping you well. It affects how you are both physically and mentally.

If you aren't getting enough sleep:

- It can make you moody and irritable and affect your relationships with your friends and family.
- Feeling tired all the time can make it difficult for you to concentrate and may affect your schoolwork.
- You are more likely to get ill if you are tired all the time.

Teenagers' sleep patterns

Research suggests that teenagers' body clocks are set later than adults' or children's. In other words, they are programmed to stay up later and to get up later. That's why they feel tired having to get up early for school, and it is important to establish a routine that gives them enough sleep.

Our sleep patterns are dictated by light and hormones. When light dims in the evening, we produce a chemical called melatonin, which tells us it's time to sleep.

The problem is that modern life has disrupted this pattern. Bright room lighting, TVs, games consoles, mobiles, tablets and PCs can all emit light that stops us producing melatonin.

So, by staying up late playing games or texting, today's teenagers are not helping themselves to get to sleep, to have enough sleep or to establish a regular sleep pattern.

(Adapted from an NHS article, 'Sleep and tiredness')

Top tips to help you get enough sleep

- Establish a routine. Go to bed at the same time each night and get up at the same time each day.

- Don't eat or drink anything immediately before you go to sleep. In particular, avoid caffeine and alcohol.

- Make sure you get out during the day and take some exercise. If you are physically tired from exercising you will get to sleep more easily.

- Switch off your mobile phone at least a quarter of an hour before you settle down. Talking to your friends will keep your brain active rather than relax you.

- Try to relax immediately before you go to sleep, for example by reading a magazine or a book, or by meditating.

- Avoid weekend lie-ins to catch up. They will just disrupt your body clock even more.

DISCUSS

Read 'Teenagers' sleep patterns', and 'Top tips to help you get enough sleep' above.

Discuss what you learn about sleep patterns.

1. Why is it important to get enough sleep?
2. Which of the top tips do you think is the most helpful?

RESEARCH

Keep a sleep diary for a week. Record the times you go to bed each night, whether you wake up during the night and for how long, what time you get up each day and how you feel each morning.

DISCUSS

Show your sleep diary to a partner. Discuss what it tells you about your sleeping habits. Can you suggest what each of you could do to enable you to get enough sleep?

15.1 Managing your emotions

Learning to control your emotions is an important life skill.

Emotions are what we feel. We usually say that we feel them in our heart, although sometimes we get strong messages or feelings from our gut (see Unit 10). Sometimes the emotions are positive and sometimes they are negative. Controlling your emotions is an important skill as it determines what emotional state you are in, which in turn determines your reactions to different events, situations and problems. This skill develops as you grow older, and is one you can always practise and improve upon.

DISCUSS

In pairs, discuss:

1. Positive feelings you can think of.

2. Negative feelings you can think of.

3. Make a list, and then rank them in order of what you think are the easiest and hardest emotions to control.

Heart to heart

Sometimes you will walk into a room and notice that you immediately like or dislike different people in the room. You may also think that the room has an 'atmosphere'. You're not imagining things. Instead, your body is feeling the energy that other people are projecting in the room – the electrical field that is generated from people's hearts.

You may also notice a person's body language. The vast majority of communication isn't about what we say, but how we say it and the body language that goes with it. If a person makes eye contact with you, comes up to you, smiles, and looks interested in what you are saying, they are acting positively towards you.

DISCUSS

Imagine you are in a room, and think one person is acting negatively towards another person. What clues give you this impression?

Being in the right mood

To make the most of different situations you need to be in the right mood or state. In a lesson, you will want to be curious, to learn what your teacher is teaching you, and to put new ideas together. In a sports lesson, you will want to be excited and energetic. You may want to be competitive if you are playing in a team sport, trying to beat another team. In an exam, you will want to be calm, focused and determined, to make sure you can score the best marks. Recognising and controlling what state you are in is key to getting the most out of situations.

DISCUSS

In pairs, consider the list of emotions below. Decide which emotions are best in the following situations:

- an academic lesson
- a sports lesson
- an exam.

Give reasons for your views.

happiness, enthusiasm, curiosity, excitement, creativity, wonder, determination, calmness, focus

When positive emotions are too much

As a rule, it's good to have positive feelings, but not too much of them. Being curious in a lesson is a good idea, but being curious about everything and asking too many questions can be annoying, disrespect people's privacy and even be dangerous in some situations (think about being too curious in the science lab).

Similarly, we all know people who are energetic and enthusiastic, but sometimes they are too energetic or enthusiastic. They always come out with an answer in class before anyone else has the chance to participate. Or they dominate a conversation, talking over other people's ideas and not letting them have a chance to express themselves.

By contrast, a person who is feeling depressed or low may need to pick themselves up and get out of their bad mood. Fortunately, there are many different ways of controlling your emotional state, including the suggestions below.

Breaking the pattern

Breaking the pattern is about doing something different to change the state you are in. Sometimes you will feel tired after completing a piece of homework, so you could get up to make yourself a cup of tea or have a snack. Sometimes you will be in an argument with someone, so you could go off to calm down and do something else. Then, once you are both calm, you can discuss the situation with the other person rationally. Sometimes you will be feeling low or depressed, so it would be a good idea to go out and get some physical exercise – even a short walk will help to change your mood.

Some people use food to change their mood. You need to be careful of doing this because, while it is a good strategy in the short term, in the long term it can lead to dietary and health problems, so you should only do it occasionally (see Unit 13).

DISCUSS

How often do you think people use food to change their mood? What could they do instead? Give reasons for your views.

What works for you?

Look at the following statements.

'I think about whether I will care about something in five years time. Usually I won't and that helps me calm down.'

'I have to go and do something physical, in order to get the adrenaline out of my body, which is what is hyping me up. I find going for a run is best.'

'I think about what really calms me. For me, it's a memory of being on holiday in Scotland, sitting by a river, on a warm sunny day. Everyone should have their own calm memory.'

'I find going for a walk works best.'

'I like to get somebody else's point of view – to help calm me down from the outside – so talking to friends is good.'

'If I'm in an argument, I try to think about things from the other person's point of view.'

DISCUSS

1. Which do you think are the best ways of controlling your emotions? Rank them in order of effectiveness. Give reasons for your views.

2. With a partner, discuss what you have learned about statement management and how to control your feelings from these pages. Do you think you will start to use these methods yourself?

WRITE

Write one or two paragraphs in your own words saying what you have learned about state management.

15.2 Managing grief

Grief is a feeling of sorrow and loss over a long period of time. This can be caused by someone's death.

People may feel grief in a variety of different situations. It can be felt when someone you know has died. It can also be felt in a family when a couple divorce – the feeling that the marriage has been lost.

If you recognise these feelings, and how they have developed, you will be able to manage them better.

DISCUSS

In groups, look at the different ways of dealing with grief. Which ones do you think are the best? Give reasons for your views.

1. 'My dad said you should never cry, but be a man, and keep it bottled up.' Dave, Plymouth

2. 'At my church, there was always a wake when somebody died, so we could sit round, talk, and remember them.' Mary, Carlisle

3. 'In my culture, the funeral is always as soon as possible after someone dies. So we'll mourn them intensely for several days. After that, your feelings gradually die down.' Nazma, Bradford

4. 'We'd get together, sing songs, and share the best stories of the person who'd died.' Benjamin, London

5. 'There's nothing like a good cry.' Ruth, Nottingham

6. 'You should respect someone when they have died, and light a candle to honour their memory.' Habeeb, Liverpool

Grief can affect all parts of our personality, and the way we behave. In order to deal with a death, it is important to know that there is a grief cycle, which most people go through. However, everyone is different and we all go through the stages at different rates. It is not a one-way process.

1. Denial

The first stage of the grief cycle is denial. In your head, you may avoid the issue completely, either by not thinking about the situation, or by imagining that the person is still alive. Your heart may feel a mixture of confusion and elation. In your gut, you may feel a combination of shock and fear that the same could happen to you.

Even though the person may have been ill for some time, their death can come suddenly. If the person has died in a sudden accident, or when they were very young, the shock can be even greater. Being in shock and denial is a defence mechanism, a natural way of protecting ourselves from being overwhelmed by too many painful feelings.

2. Anger

The second stage of the grief cycle is anger. The emotional response goes upwards, so you might temporarily feel better but very angry after a death. This is natural, but it is one of the most difficult feelings to admit to. During this stage, you need to be careful not to direct your anger at others, such as the doctors and nurses who tried to save the dead person, other adults, the family of the dead person or even the dead person themselves.

It is important to note that anger is only harmful if you take it out on other people or yourself. Over time, the anger will diminish.

3. Bargaining

This is when you try to come to terms with the situation emotionally, by bargaining with yourself. This can lead to resentment, as you realise the situation is real. You may try to kid yourself that the death does not mean that much or, for an older person, that they lived a full and happy life. This is only bargaining because ultimately you still have to go through other stages in the grief process.

4. Depression

This is the lowest point of the grief cycle, and can last some time. This is when the fact of the death has really hit home. At this point you can feel guilty that you are still alive, while the other person has died. It is important to work through this depression – to keep on exercising, seeing friends, doing activities, going out and living a normal life, even though you may not like feel doing so. Eventually the depression will pass.

5. Acceptance

This is the final stage of the grief cycle, where you begin to feel better. You may always feel a little sad about a person's death, but you are able to manage it and go on normally day to day.

DISCUSS

Discuss each stage of the grief cycle.

1. Which do you feel would be the most difficult to deal with?

2. Which is the easiest to get your head around?

Give reasons for your views.

Showing emotions

Sometimes, it is difficult to show your emotions. For example, boys are sometimes taught not to cry at a young age. You might find it difficult to share your emotions with a group of friends if you think they might be unsympathetic. However, a good friend will allow their friends to share and show their negative emotions.

Crying is one way to show grief, but there are many other ways. Thinking about the person you miss, talking about them with family or friends, writing about them, reliving memories on social media – there is a long list of different things you could do to express your grief.

YOUR CHOICE

In pairs, consider the following emotions and the different ways of dealing with them. Match the emotion to the best way of dealing with it.

1. Anger

2. Depression

3. Guilt

4. Resentment

5. Sadness

6. Shock

a) Getting out, having some exercise or seeing some friends to take your mind off things.

b) Working through the problem logically with a teacher, coach or counsellor until you realise it's not your fault.

c) Talking through your feelings with someone understanding, until you accept the situation.

d) Remembering the person you've lost by having a good cry.

e) Sitting down, having a glass of water, a cup of tea or coffee, or something to eat.

f) Going to a boxing ring and hitting something until you feel better.

15.3 Dealing with divorce or parents splitting up

When parents separate or divorce, it is often difficult for children to deal with.

Loss can affect us in many different ways. When a situation changes, such as a person leaving us or when a family splits up, we miss the emotional connection we once had. Loss can change the way we think about things. In severe cases, loss can change our very identity – how we view ourselves.

Sometimes parents will choose to divorce or split up. This can be difficult for everyone. It is important to recognise that different people react to divorce and family break-ups in different ways.

How to tell kids about divorce: An age-by-age guide

The news that Mom and Dad are separating hits a two-year-old and a 10-year-old differently. Here's how to help children handle it at any age.

Erica Hallman of Toronto recalls her daughter Jessica, then in kindergarten, trying to understand the conflicts behind her parents' separation. 'One time she asked me, "Why are you fighting? Is it because he deleted something from your computer?" This misunderstanding was easily remedied. Yes, Dad had deleted something from Mom's computer and they had angry words about it, but, of course, that did not cause the divorce. However, her daughter's question made

Hallman realise Jessica's need to make sense of circumstances she couldn't fully understand.

School-aged children may show their distress as fear, anxiety, anger or sadness, and some display more clear-cut signs of missing their absent parent. Some may have fantasies about reconciliation and wonder what they can do to make that happen. One expert says, 'Children who think that they might be able to bring their parents back together, or that they somehow contributed to the divorce, will have trouble getting on with the healing process. So they need to understand that those are adult decisions which they didn't cause and can't influence.'

John Hoffman, May 1, 2018, todaysparent.com

ROLE PLAY

In pairs, act out a scene in which two friends discuss the difficulties they are experiencing because their parents are in the process of splitting up.

DISCUSS

Study the advice below for children on how to deal with divorce.

1. In pairs, discuss which you feel are the most helpful. Rank them in order of preference.

2. Then discuss your list with another pair. Give reasons for your views.

   a) 'Time heals. The important thing is to allow yourself to process all of your emotions, and be honest to yourself.' Jasmine, Birmingham

   b) 'Children have a tendency to blame one of the parents, when often the truth is that it's nobody's fault. So avoid blaming people.' Mohammed, London

   c) 'Communication is key. Now it's even more important to treat each parent separately and make it very clear what you want and expect out of the situation, while accepting you will not all be living together.' Jacob, Manchester.

   d) 'Children aged eight or over often have a great support network, and so should talk to their friends, coaches and teachers about their feelings, as well as their parents.' Lucy, Bristol

   e) 'It's OK to have a preference about which parent you want to live with.' Alice, Newcastle

   f) 'Avoid getting caught in the middle of your parents' argument.' Danny, Cardiff

   g) 'You're not to blame – it's your parents' relationship.' Katie, Plymouth

Dealing with the loss

Like a death, a divorce or parents splitting up can bring a strong sense of loss, and you will go through stages of the grief cycle (see pages 78–79). What is being lost can vary – it can be a sense of identity from the old family unit, access to one parent and possibly siblings, financial resources and a feeling of peace that comes when you are in a stable, long-term family unit.

There are people who can help you to deal with the loss, such as each of your parents, your grandparents, friends, teachers, coaches and counsellors. You can decide who you would feel most comfortable talking to about the situation. You may find that different people can help you at different times.

DISCUSS

Imagine that a friend had one of the following problems due to their parents splitting up. Who would you get them to go and speak to, and why? Give reasons for your views.

1. 'I'm not sure who is going to be looking after me now that they are splitting up.'

2. 'I'm having trouble concentrating on my school work because mum and dad are arguing.'

3. 'I'm feeling very lonely and like I can't talk to my parents.'

4. 'Family is very important to me. I want to make sure I carry on seeing both sets of grandparents.'

5. 'Will I still live with my brother or sister?'

6. 'This is really upsetting – I feel down and depressed all of the time.'

Ask Erica

Dear Erica

My mum and dad are getting divorced. Dad blames Mum for their splitting up because she had an affair and has gone to live with Tony. Dad tries to stop us going round to their house. But my brother and I want to see Mum and we get on well with Tony. What can we do? Can he stop us seeing her?

Rashida

WRITE

Write Erica's reply to Rashida.

Counsellors

Sometimes people feel broken-hearted and their very sense of identity or wellbeing can be affected. In these cases, it might be appropriate to seek professional help from a counsellor. This is someone independent who you can to talk to about the issues affecting you.

Your school may well have a counsellor, or there may be one attached to your doctor's surgery. If you do feel you need someone professional to talk to about your problems, tell a responsible adult who you know, trust and feel comfortable with. 81

16.1 Pocket money

Learning to manage your money is a vital skill.

Many children are given pocket money by their parents or carers. You may be given a regular amount of money each week or month. Some families don't give pocket money regularly. They will give money when you ask for it, or when they can afford it.

There is no law saying that parents must give children pocket money. Nor do parents have to give children a certain amount of pocket money.

Read what one parent has to say:

'I'd give my children pocket money, if I could, but I can't afford it.'
Single mother of three

DISCUSS

Whatever pocket money you get, remember: 'Money doesn't grow on trees'.

Discuss what this means.

Should you have to earn your pocket money?

In many families, children have to earn their pocket money by doing chores.

'I don't think payment for chores is a good idea. It's kind of a bribe. Children need to learn that household tasks are part of daily living and aren't a job you do to earn money.'
Mother of two

'I give my 11-year-old up to £5 a week, provided he does his chores and behaves himself.'
Father of 11-year-old

DISCUSS

1. In groups, make a list of household chores.

2. Think about chores that have to be done whether you like doing them or not. Then discuss the questions below.

   a) Which chores would you be willing to do in return for payment?

   b) Are there any tasks that everyone in the household should share without being paid for doing them?

   c) Should you have to do chores in order to earn your pocket money? If so, what do you think you should get for each of the chores on the list?

   d) Should you lose pocket money for bad behaviour, such as being rude, getting into trouble at school or not doing your homework? Is it right for parents to use stopping pocket money as a punishment?

   e) Should you be able to earn more pocket money as a reward for working hard at school or for doing well in tests at school? Should you only be paid if you get good results?

3. Discuss the idea of having a pocket money contract. In it, you and your parents or carers specify what your pocket money is to be used for, and agree what you are going to do in return for getting pocket money. The contract will also specify whether there are any circumstances in which your pocket money will be stopped.

   Draw up a contract and then share your ideas in a class discussion.

Fact check

A survey of what children aged 7–15 spend their money on found:

- Clothes and shoes were the items on which the most money was spent.
- Boys spent ten times as much as girls on computer games and software.
- Girls spent twice as much on books.
- Seventeen per cent of girls bought at least one item of toiletries or cosmetics per fortnight compared with two per cent of boys.
- More than half bought at least one soft drink per fortnight.

DISCUSS

Imagine you have £10 a week to spend. Study the lists below and decide how you would spend it and whether you would save some of it.

Things you might spend it on: sweets, snacks and soft drinks; comics and/or magazines; going out, e.g. to the cinema; toiletries and cosmetics; music, apps or computer games.

Things you might save it for: top-up for your mobile; to help buy a big item for your birthday; to pay for presents for your family, e.g. their birthdays or festivals such as Christmas and Divali.

Ask Erica

Dear Erica

I don't know what to do. I borrowed some money from my friend's older brother to buy this computer game. Now he's asking for it back, but I haven't got it to give him. He says if I don't pay him at once, he'll start charging interest. What does he mean? Can he do that?

Sean

Dear Erica

A group of us planned to go to the cinema. One of my friends said they hadn't got enough cash left so I lent them the money. That was three weeks ago and they still haven't paid me back. What can I do?

Sam

Dear Erica

I get £5 a week every Monday but I've spent it all by Wednesday. Can you give me any advice on what I can do about it?

Izzy

Money management tips

If you run out of money before the end of the week, it is usually because you haven't planned your spending carefully enough.

Three things you can do are:

1. Plan ahead. Work out what you are going to spend your money on (see 'Budgeting' on the next page).

2. Stick to the plan. Don't buy something on impulse. That pack of doughnuts may look tempting, but was it listed in your plan?

3. Arrange for your money to be paid in instalments. For example, you could get half on Sunday and half on Wednesday.

WRITE

Write Erica's replies to Sean, Sam and Izzy.

DISCUSS

Compare your advice in a class discussion.

16.2 Budgeting

A budget is a plan which helps you to manage your money by keeping track of how much you have (your income) and how much you spend (your expenses).

Needs and wants

Start by thinking about what you will use your money for. Work out your spending priorities: what you actually need and what you would like to have.

WRITE

1. Begin by listing all the things you *need* that have to be paid for by someone, at home and at school.

   Here is Sam's list:

   > **Home:** food, clothes, heating, lighting, water, toiletries, haircuts, transport, wireless internet.

   > **School:** uniform, sports kit, stationery, books, mobile phone (for calculator and kahoots!), lunches.

2. Now list all the things you *want*: things you would like to have but which aren't essential needs.

   Here is Sam's list:

   > Trendy clothes and trainers, meals out, make-up, holidays, school trips, cinema and concert tickets, extra data for surfing social media on phone, extra texts, movie and series pass on TV, Netflix.

YOUR CHOICE

3. Study your list of needs. Who should pay for them, you or your parents/carer? Are there any you think should be shared?

4. Now study your list of wants. Who should be responsible for paying for each of these?

DISCUSS

Below is Sam's monthly budget for income. In pairs, look at the income. Can you think of any other ways that Sam could make some more money? How might Sam's budget for next month look different in December?

Income:	
Pocket money 4 x £6.50	£26
Money for extra chores (5 done)	£14
Money from Grandma	£10
Total:	£50

Necessities and luxuries

A necessity is something that you need to survive day to day. Necessities might include food or housing (the 'needs' listed above). By contrast, a luxury is something that you don't necessarily need, but you desire to improve your life, such as a meal out, or a cinema ticket, or extra data for your mobile phone (the 'wants' listed above).

DISCUSS

1. Look at the list below.

  a) Which items do you think are necessities?

  b) Which items do you think are luxuries?

  Give reasons for your views.

> clean drinking water   fizzy drinks   fruit and vegetables   a meal out   junk food
> make-up   a mobile phone   tampons
> a haircut   a bus pass to get to school
> wireless internet   a TV

2. Below is Sam's monthly budget for expenditure. In groups, look at what Sam is spending the money on. Where do you think Sam can save some money? Give reasons for your views.

Expenditure:	
Fizzy drinks (1 per school day at £1 each)	£20
Extra data for mobile phone	£10
Cinema twice per month (£5 on Tuesdays)	£10
Heating, electricity, water, food at home	£0 (paid for by parents)
Make-up	£10
Concert (none this month)	£0

Savings can be the difference between income and expenditure. How much money can Sam save this month?

DISCUSS

Look again as Sam's expenditure budget. What do you think has been missed out? What do you think Sam should add to the budget? Give reasons for your views.

Opportunity costs

Opportunity cost was discussed in Unit 10.2. It is the price of the next best alternative when you buy something which you miss out on. To buy a concert ticket for £12, Sam would have to save some money elsewhere. What would you save from Sam's expenditure budget?

Short- and long-run costs

Short-run costs are things that you have to pay for in the short run, such as every day or every week. They can include food, bus trips, or a can of fizzy drink.

Long-run costs are things that you don't have to pay for in the short run. However, in the long run, you wouldn't be able to live without them. For example, Sam hasn't included a replacement mobile phone in the budget, which may be needed in the long run.

WRITE

Look at the lists of Sam's needs and wants. Divide up all these goods into short-run goods and long-run goods. Then compare your list with a partner. Give reasons for your views.

The bank of Mum and Dad

Look again at Sam's budget. You will see that there are many things which are paid for by Sam's parents. This can include rent or a mortgage for their house or flat, a TV licence, water, gas and electricity, wireless internet, a phone bill, and all the food and drink that you consume at home.

RESEARCH

Make a list of your parents' budget, and estimate how much you think they are paying to support you each week. The number might surprise you. Then think about what they expect in return – such as good behaviour at home and school, and homework completed on time. Do you think you are a good investment?

17.1 How you spend your time

Surveys suggest that young people are not making the most of their leisure time.

Do you make the best use of your leisure time?

Do this quiz to find out whether you make the best use of your leisure time. Think about what you do and how you spend your time on an average day after school. Keep a record of your answers and check what they say about how you use your leisure time.

Quiz

How much time do you spend each day:

1. Surfing the internet:
   a) less than half an hour
   b) up to 1 hour
   c) more than an hour?

2. Playing video games:
   a) up to half an hour
   b) up to 2 hours
   c) 2 hours or more?

3. Texting your friends:
   a) less than an hour
   b) 1–2 hours
   c) more than 2 hours?

4. On your hobby:
   a) none
   b) up to an hour
   c) more than an hour?

5. Earning pocket-money by doing chores:
   a) none
   b) up to 15 minutes
   c) over 15 minutes?

6. Alone in your bedroom:
   a) half an hour
   b) up to 3 hours
   c) 3 hours or more?

7. Out of doors:
   a) none
   b) up to an hour
   c) more than an hour?

8. Taking part in a sport or other physical activity:
   a) none
   b) up to an hour
   c) more than an hour?

9. Watching TV or a film:
   a) up to an hour
   b) 1–2 hours
   c) more than 2 hours?

10. Reading a book:
    a) none
    b) up to an hour
    c) more than an hour?

11. Hanging about outside with your friends:
    a) none
    b) up to an hour
    c) more than an hour?

12. Feeling bored:
    a) none
    b) less than quarter of an hour
    c) more than quarter of an hour?

What your answers say about how you spend your leisure time

Questions 1 and 2: If you answered **a)** to both these questions, then you are spending a limited amount of time on the computer. But if you answered **b)**, you need to consider whether you are spending too much time browsing and gaming. And if you answered **c)** and are spending 3–4 hours a day on the computer, you need to think seriously about cutting down, especially on gaming, which can become addictive.

Question 3: If you answered **a)** your use of your phone is under control, but if you answered **b)** or **c)** you need to think about whether you are using it too much.

Question 4: If you answered **b)** or **c)** you are spending your time more effectively than those who answered **a)**, who either haven't got a hobby or don't spend much time on it.

Question 5: If you answered **a)** you may be missing an opportunity to increase your pocket money. if you answered **b)** or **c)** you are aware of the opportunity that doing extra chores offers.

Question 6: If you answered **b)** or **c)** you are in danger of becoming isolated. You need to think about spending more time with your family and friends.

Question 7: If you answered **a)** or **b)** you should think about getting out more.

Question 8: If you answered **a)** then you should think about getting more exercise.

Question 9: If you answered **c)** you need to think whether you spend too much time watching TV when you could be being more active.

Question 10: Many people find reading enjoyable, informative and relaxing. If you answered **a)** you may be missing out on an activity which you could benefit from.

Question 11: If you answered **b)** or **c)**, at least you are seeing your friends face-to-face rather just texting them from your bedroom. If you answered **a)** you should consider going out more often.

Question 12: If you answered **a)** you are probably making good use of your time if you aren't just spending it texting or gaming or watching TV. If you answered **b)** or **c)** then you need to think about how you could spend your time more productively.

DISCUSS

In pairs, discuss what you have learned from the quiz about how you spend your leisure time. Each decide on one or two things you could do to make better use of your leisure time.

Ten ways to make better use of your leisure time

1. Spend less time playing computer games.
2. Cut down the time you spend on your mobile phone.
3. Join an after-school club.
4. Go for a walk or a bike ride.
5. Ration how much TV you watch.
6. Read a magazine or a book.
7. Learn how to cook.
8. Help out more around the house.
9. Visit an elderly relative or neighbour.
10. Take up a hobby.

WRITE

Write an article offering advice to people of your age on how to make better use of their leisure time.

17.2 Internet gaming addiction

More and more young people are becoming addicted to internet gaming.

There are two forms of internet gaming addiction, depending on whether the games involve single players or multiple players.

Single players may get addicted to trying to outperform other players of the game.

In games involving multiple players, individuals may create characters who either cooperate against an enemy or compete against each other. Players can come to believe in their on-screen characters to such an extent that they begin to feel that they are real. Taking part in the game becomes more important to them than anything else.

The signs of addiction to internet games

Emotional and mental signs:

- tiredness
- lack of interest in what family and friends are doing
- preoccupation with thoughts about the current game
- irritability if asked to stop gaming
- depression
- lying about how much time is spent gaming
- lack of interest in schoolwork.

Physical signs:

- poor eating habits – can't be bothered with meals
- migraines brought on by long periods of intense concentration, or eye strain from looking at the screen for too long
- a stiff neck
- painful thumb from continuous use of the controller, which is sometimes called 'Nintenditis'
- repetitive strain injury to nerves in the hand, known as carpal tunnel syndrome
- poor personal hygiene – can't stop to have a shower or be bothered to change clothes.

In addition, a person may get into financial trouble by overspending on the latest games and through 'in-app' purchases. In 2018, *Fortnite: Battle Royale* was free to download, but at the height of the craze was making $50 million in a single day through 'in-app' purchases, one of which, for £7.99, enabled the gamers to make their characters do dances like 'The Wiggle'.

DISCUSS

1. Should the sale of games that are age-related be more strictly controlled? The game *Grand Theft Auto* is rated as 18+ but is played by children who are much younger. How could its sale be controlled?

2. Should games that contain violence, nudity and foul language have to carry a written warning?

3. Should shops be forced to keep games out of sight in the way they do with cigarettes?

Addicted to gaming

In 2018, a 15-year-old boy became the first person diagnosed with internet gaming addiction. He was off school for a year after he lost the confidence to leave home because he was so addicted to gaming.

He spent eight weeks in hospital because he was unable to function properly. 'Every moment he's awake, he wants to be on a game,' said his mother. 'There is no outside world. It has become all-consuming.'

The World Health Organisation has classified addiction to internet gaming as a mental health disorder.

Why are games so addictive?

When you play violent video games and your character is shot at, your survival instinct takes over and tells you to fight back. Your body reacts as it would in a real-life situation. Your heartbeat races, your adrenaline spikes and stress hormones flood your body. But it is only your on-screen character who is at risk, so you can fight back and the enjoyment you get from doing so is so great it can become addictive.

Here are some opinions on why video games are bad for you.

'Children who spend too much time playing video games do not get enough exercise.'

'Violent video games make children immune to violence.'

'Violence in video games increases the risk of a person behaving violently.'

'Violent video games can give children nightmares.'

'Playing video games can be addictive.'

Here are some opinions on why video games are not bad for you.

'If you play three hours of *Call of Duty*, you may feel a little pumped, but you are not going to go out and mug somebody.'

'The evidence that violent video games lead to real-life violence is inconclusive.'

'Violent video games often involve some problem-solving. They stimulate the brain and increase intelligence.'

'People who play action-based video games are quicker at making real-life decisions.'

'Playing video games increases a person's dexterity.'

DISCUSS

Do you think the violence in computer games affects the people who play them? Do the players become immune to violence?

Ask Erica

DISCUSS

Discuss what Tania could say to her brother.

WRITE

Now write Erica's reply to Tania.

Dear Erica

I think my brother is addicted to gaming. How can I convince him to spend less time playing internet games?

Tania

18.1 Speaking your mind

Listening to the views of others can help you to clarify your own opinions.

Three examples of the way people speak their mind are: being aggressive; being manipulative; and being assertive. The first two don't take into account what other people are saying in a discussion. The third one, being assertive, does.

Aggressive speaking can include shouting, interrupting another person, stealing their ideas and making it your own (known as tailgating), bullying (see Unit 8) and personal attacks. While you might feel you have made your point, this is not a successful long-term strategy as it hurts the other person's feelings and may damage your relationship with them. They may avoid you, switch off from what you are saying and ignore your contributions in future – even when you aren't being aggressive – because of how you have treated them.

Manipulative speaking can include deliberately saying one thing when you mean another, saying one thing to one person and another thing to another, and playing on a person's emotions to get them to act in a particular way. Again, this is not a successful strategy in the long run as it ignores the other person's point of view. Manipulative behaviour destroys trust, which again means people may ignore you, switch off from what you are saying or avoid you if you gain a manipulative reputation.

Assertive behaviour is different, because you are stating your point of view from a position of strength, without ignoring other points of view in the discussion. It comes across as confident, because you acknowledge that there are other points of view, even when you feel differently. Assertive behaviour is a good way of getting your point across without damaging relationships or hurting others' feelings.

1. In pairs, look at the following examples. Decide which ones you think are aggressive, which assertive and which manipulative.

2. Then compare your answers in groups, giving reasons for your views.

3. Come up with an assertive alternative to each example of aggressive or manipulative behaviour.

a) 'I can't believe that you've cheated. You're a liar and a cheat. I'm so angry with you.'

b) 'From my point of view, it looks like you've said one thing, but that something else has occurred. Can you explain to me what's going on please, because I'm quite hurt?'

c) 'Ah, bless you, you would say that wouldn't you? However, I was talking with Beth, Fred and Johnny and they all agree with my point of view, so I think you should too.'

d) 'I think we need to talk this over further. I had a look over your proposal, but I've been thinking about a different way of doing things. Perhaps we could merge our ideas together?'

e) 'No, I'm not listening to anything you say now. I'm right, you're wrong. How could you do this?'

f) 'Shut up. I was speaking first, so now you're going to listen.'

g) 'Yeah, men talk like that all the time. You'd never hear that from a woman, would you?'

h) 'OK, let's slow down and discuss this together. You want to look forward on this; I want to look backwards. Let's see if we can work this out together.'

Speaking in groups

Sometimes you may be asked to take part in a group discussion. Often, this will be in the classroom. However, you also may find yourself in a natural discussion with your friends. Later on in life, you might find yourself in a formal group discussion at work. Therefore, it's important to know what the rules of a group discussion are, and to make sure that you take part.

When you take part in a group discussion, make sure you do the following things:

- Understand what the discussion is about. The teacher has said talk about the news, but different people may interpret this differently. One person may talk about the sports news, another about current affairs, and another about the latest news from a reality TV show like *Love Island*. So it's important to understand what the discussion is going to be about. If somebody has set you a group discussion as a task and you're not sure what it's meant to be about, ask for clarification.

- Recognise what sort of conversation you are in. Is it formal or informal? Is everyone going to speak in turn, or can you interrupt or ask questions? If people are speaking in turns, wait your turn. What are the unspoken rules to the discussion?

- Make sure you join in. Teachers, employers and recruiters all like people who join in. So make sure that you have something to say, even if it's only one comment, by making a point, clearly and confidently.

- Listen carefully to everyone who is speaking. That way you are able to follow the direction the conversation is taking. This is especially important when listening to people who disagree with you. That way, you will learn the main arguments against your point of view, and you may even learn something or change your mind in the process.

- Make sure you and others stick to the point of the discussion. If you find yourself wandering off topic – stop, apologise and then go back on topic. If somebody else is wandering off topic, politely point this out.

- Give reasons. If you are arguing a point of view, give good valid reasons to make your point. Make sure these are true. If you are not sure, say so.

1. Take it in turns to talk about the best discussions you've ever had. What was the situation? Why were these discussions good?

2. Make a list of rules for the best discussions you've ever had. Then compare your list with another group. Give reasons for your views.

In pairs, imagine you are a parent discussing with a teenager your concerns about them spending too much time on their mobile phone.

18.2 Listening and giving feedback

Effective listening is a skill you need to develop in order to be successful.

Listening to others

Because there is so much knowledge in our society, it is impossible to learn everything. The key skill, then, is being able to access the specialist knowledge that other people have, whether this is through your teachers, your parents, your siblings, your friends or an expert. Effective listening is a key part of this.

In order to be an effective listener, follow these guidelines:

1. Keep silent. It's OK to nod in agreement, or say 'Yes' or 'Um' in agreement. However, it's important not to interrupt. Respect what the other person is saying. You can always make your point once they have finished.

2. Keep some eye contact, but avoid staring into their eyes all the time. Instead, face the person who is speaking and make regular eye contact, to show that you are interested in what they are saying.

3. Stay in rapport with the person. This can involve matching or mirroring their posture, nodding in agreement with what they are saying, and showing an interest in what they are saying.

4. Give feedback. If someone is speaking too fast or you can't hear them, or the language is too technical, tell them. The speaker wants you to understand what they are saying. They can only correct a problem if you tell them what it is.

5. If a speaker asks for questions at the end of a presentation, ask an intelligent question. This shows that you have listened and taken a genuine interest in the subject.

Think of a person who is a really good listener.

1. What do they do that makes them a good listener?

2. What other things can you think of that makes an effective listener?

Compare your answers with those of other groups.

Think about a time when you really listened to a speaker.

1. Why did you really listen to them?

2. What could you do to listen more in the future?

3. Make an action plan of what you are going to do to really listen in the future.

Giving and receiving feedback

After a task like public speaking, it is important that you can give and receive feedback in order to improve in the future. However, there are some rules to feedback that you should follow, in order to make the feedback safe and effective.

Rules for giving feedback

1. Wait for the person who has just completed the task to ask for feedback. Sometimes feedback may not be appropriate – the person may have something else going on in their lives, like a family emergency. Wait for them to come to you.

    Note: feedback should always be face to face in order to be genuine and productive.

2. Ask the person first: 'What do you think went well?'

    Often people will know what went well, and will be able to identify their own points for feedback. So, rather than taking over, let them talk about what went well. Allow them to continue in some depth with this. After they've made their first point, ask them, 'What else went well?' Continue to do this to build their confidence.

    Once they have finished describing what went well, add in your own points of what went well.

3. Then ask the person: 'What are you going to improve for next time?'

    Note: ideally neither of you should use negatives. Instead, you must focus either on the positives for this time, or what positive behaviour will occur next time.

4. Next, ask: 'How are you going to improve for next time?' and 'Are there any resources you need to help you to succeed?' This will get them thinking about how to improve, and to identify any barriers and how to overcome these by applying extra resources to them.

5. Spend more time on the positives than on the negatives. The ratio should be four to five positives for every one negative. This is the ratio psychologists have discovered help us to grow and develop as individuals.

Look at the following list of examples. How would you give feedback in the following situations?

1. A member of your class is quite athletic, and enjoys sports. However, when playing football they tend to dominate and hog the ball. Your team mates are getting annoyed about this.

2. A close friend has started experimenting with make-up. However, they are using far too much of it and other people in your class are laughing at them behind their back.

3. A member of your family is spending way too much time on social media. It's beginning to affect their school work.

4. A member of your class has some really good points to make in a forthcoming debate. However, they are quite shy and don't like public speaking.

5. A member of your family always shouts when they get up in the morning, even when nothing is wrong. Other members of your family don't like it.

6. A close friend is spending a lot more time with their partner, and none at all with you – despite you being best friends. You're starting to feel awkward about it.

In pairs, think about a time you both did public speaking in class. Give and receive feedback with your partner. Make an action plan for how you are going to improve your public speaking.

Now write a summary of how you think the feedback went. Keep a journal so that you are always improving the feedback you give, and how you respond to feedback from others in the future.

7. Sometimes it will be necessary to give and receive feedback in a group. What do you think are the advantages and disadvantages of doing this? Give reasons for your views.

19.1 Being a good neighbour

Getting to know the people who live around you and taking care of the local area can strengthen your sense of pride in your neighbourhood.

What is a neighbour?

A neighbour is somebody who lives in your local area, or neighbourhood. They could live right next door, or in the same block of flats, or on your street. Or they could live a short distance away from you. Although they live near you, they could be very different in their background and the way that they live their lives.

In groups, look at the following statements. Discuss which ones you agree with and why. Give reasons for your views.

1. 'A good neighbour keeps themselves to themselves, and doesn't bother anyone else.'

2. 'A good neighbour will keep an eye out. If some kids break one of your windows, and a neighbour sees it, they will tell you who did it and help you report it to the police.'

3. 'A good neighbour will let you borrow their lawnmower or patio sprayer for free, for as long as you like.'

4. 'A good neighbour gets involved in their community, through things like Neighbourhood Watch or litter picking in the local park.'

5. 'A good neighbour doesn't challenge you on things like loud music or whether you've overfilled the bins and put rubbish bags around them which won't be collected.'

Neighbourhood Watch

Neighbourhood Watch is a scheme set up by neighbours to improve their area by watching out for problems, especially crimes or suspicious activity, which can then be reported to the police. The police work closely with Neighbourhood Watch schemes. The first Neighbourhood Watch scheme in the UK was set up in Cheshire, in 1982, following the success of a similar scheme in the USA.

Neighbourhood Watch schemes are successful because they rely on local people's knowledge. They are so successful that some house insurance companies offer cheaper insurance to those people who live in a Neighbourhood Watch area.

In pairs, think about what would make the perfect neighbour.

- What would they do?
- How would they behave?
- How would they treat you?

Then think about how you could be the perfect neighbour.

- What would you do?
- How would you behave?
- How would you treat other people?

Give reasons for your views.

Does your neighbourhood have a Neighbourhood Watch scheme? Use the internet and local knowledge to see if the Neighbourhood Watch symbol appears anywhere in your local area. If so, contact them and find out what they do. If not, contact your local councillor and/or local MP and ask whether there should be a Neighbourhood Watch scheme in your area.

Improving your neighbourhood

Sometimes there will be things wrong with your neighbourhood. A fence or signpost may be broken, a pond may be covered in weeds, or there may be a high rate of crime.

Some of these problems are more serious that others, and different people are responsible for dealing with different issues.

In pairs: Look at the following problems below and decide who is responsible for dealing with them. The people who can deal with them are you, your neighbours, you and your neighbours, Neighbourhood Watch, the police, the local council and your local MP. Then compare your answers in groups. Your teacher will then provide you with a list of the correct answers.

Problems in your area:

1. Too many potholes in the road.

2. Your rubbish isn't being picked up by the local council because you've overfilled the bins.

3. People are dumping rubbish in the local street, and the police have no idea who it is.

4. A fence is broken between your house and next door.

5. Your neighbour's tree has grown over your fence and is now growing above your garden. It is blocking the light to your lawn, which is dying.

6. The street sign at the end of your road is broken.

7. Public trees and flower beds in your neighbourhood are dying because of a long hot summer and lack of water.

8. Your neighbour keeps parking outside your house all day, and you don't have a drive. They do, and it's empty.

Street scene champions

Many local councils now have schemes in which members of the public can volunteer to help improve their local area. These are usually called 'local environment champions' or 'street scene champions'. Oxford City Council is one area with such a scheme. These local champions do the following:

- pick up litter

- clean up graffiti where it isn't wanted

- report the illegal dumping of rubbish, known as fly tipping

- report flyposting, where people put up posters illegally

- report dog-fouling and challenge people when they catch them doing it

- encourage recycling at home, at work and in their local community

- work with the council to improve local air quality

- report potholes

- campaign for better cycling facilities and public transport.

In pairs, rank the problems listed above in the order of priority in which you would deal with them. Then compare your answers with another pair. Give reasons for your views.

In groups, discuss what you think of 'street scene champions'.

1. Are they a good idea? Or are they interfering busybodies who should mind their own business?

2. Should they be helping the council? Or should the council be paying people to fix the things they are responsible for themselves?

20.1 First aid: what to do in an emergency

Knowing how to give first aid can help you to deal with accidents.

First aid for falls

- If someone has fallen, approach them calmly and reassuringly, but be alert to any danger to you or them.
- Do not move the person if the injury looks serious. This is particularly important if the neck or spine is injured, because damage to the spinal cord can cause paralysis.
- Call an ambulance. While you are waiting for it, keep the person warm and talk to them. Do not give them anything to drink in case they need to be given an anaesthetic later.

First aid for burns and scalds

Burns and scalds damage the skin and destroy the blood vessels beneath the skin. The first aid treatment is the same for burns and scalds.

1. Remove anything tight such as a wristwatch or jewellery, as burned skin often swells up.
2. Cool the burn under cold running water for at least ten minutes. This will reduce the pain, swelling and risk of scarring.
3. Once the burn has cooled, cover it with clingfilm or a clean unused plastic bag. This will help to protect the skin from infection.
4. If the person is badly burned or scalded, call an ambulance.

DO NOT:

- try to pull off any clothing that is stuck to the skin
- put any cream or ointment on the skin
- use anything fluffy such as cotton wool to clean the skin
- prick any blisters.

First aid for cuts

If someone loses too much blood their body will not get enough oxygen. Severe blood loss can cause death, so if someone is bleeding badly, you must try to stop the bleeding while an ambulance is called.

Put pressure on the wound to stop or slow down the flow of blood.

If you can, raise the injured part above the level of the casualty's chest. This slows down the blood flow from the heart to the injured part.

A large cut may require stitches. Don't try to clean it or to remove any object embedded in the wound. Removing it can cause more damage and increase the blood flow, as the object may be plugging the wound.

First aid for suffocation and choking

If someone is suffocating, remove what is causing the suffocation. If the person has stopped breathing, they may need CPR (cardiopulmonary resuscitation). Call an ambulance.

Someone who is choking may be clutching at their chest or neck and won't be able to speak, breathe or cough.

- If the person choking is an adult, stand behind them and slightly to one side. Put a hand on their chest and lean them forwards, then give them five blows between the shoulders with the heel of your hand.
- If the person choking is a child over 1 year, lean the child over your knee or bend them forwards, so the head is lower than the chest. Give five firm blows between the shoulder blades with the palm of your hand.

- If this doesn't dislodge the object that is making them choke, stand behind them, and with one hand make a fist. Put your arm round them so the fist is just above their belly button. Put your other hand round them and grasp the fist. Pull hard on the fist five times, giving abdominal thrusts which should remove the object.

- If a baby is choking, hold it face down along your thigh, with its head lower than its bottom. Support its head and pat it firmly on the back between the shoulders five times.

First aid for head injuries

A blow to the head can be serious.

- If the person is unconscious, call an ambulance. Check that they are breathing and if so, put them in the recovery position, keeping them warm while you wait for the ambulance.

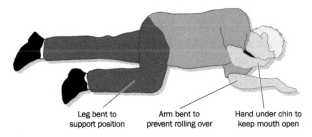

Leg bent to support position   Arm bent to prevent rolling over   Hand under chin to keep mouth open

- If they are conscious, applying something cold to the injury will reduce external swelling and pain.

- If they start to feel drowsy or to vomit, they may have concussion. This can be serious and you should call an ambulance.

- Other signs of concussion are: being unresponsive, dizziness, headache, being confused, blurred vision, having no memory of the incident.

First aid for shock

A person who has had a serious injury may be suffering from shock, which can cause unconsciousness and even death. Symptoms vary depending on how severe the shock is. They include paleness, feeling faint, cold and clammy skin, a weak and fast pulse, fast and shallow breathing and confusion.

- Lay the person down with their head low and their legs raised and supported, but do not move them if you think it may cause further injuries.

- Loosen any tight clothing around the neck, chest and waist to make sure it doesn't constrict their blood flow.

- Call an ambulance and keep the person warm and comfortable while you wait.

DISCUSS

In pairs, discuss these questions.

1. Why is it dangerous to move someone who may have injured their neck or spine? What first aid should you give to someone who has had a fall?

2. How would you try to stop bleeding from a cut?

3. How would you treat a wound with an object embedded in it?

4. How would you treat a burn? What is it wrong to do when you are treating a burn? Explain why.

5. What would you do if someone choked on a boiled sweet?

6. Why is concussion dangerous? How can you tell if a person is concussed?

WRITE

Write your answers to the questions you discussed.

Ask Erica

Dear Erica
How can I tell if someone is suffering from shock? What should I do if I think they are in shock?

Jo

WRITE

Write Erica's reply.

ROLE PLAY

In pairs, use the information on this page to produce a sketch for a children's television programme in which a character called Donald Doitright is given advice by a character called Felicity the First Aider. Try to make the sketch humorous, while conveying important advice.

Acknowledgments

The publishers gratefully acknowledge the permission granted to reproduce the copyright material in this book. Every effort has been made to trace copyright holders and to obtain their permission for the use of copyright material. The publishers will gladly receive any information enabling them to rectify any error or omission at the first opportunity.

Images

Key: t = top, b = bottom, l = left, r = right, c = centre.

p6 travelstock44/Alamy Stock Photo, p7 bikeworldtravel/Shutterstock, p9 t Kzenon/Shutterstock, p9 b Monkey Business Images/Shutterstock, p10 Contraband Collection/Alamy Stock Photo, p11 t grebeshkovmaxim/Shutterstock, p11 b Barnaby Chambers/Shutterstock, p12 Iakov Filimonov/Shutterstock, p13 t Borislav Bajkic/Shutterstock, p13 b Alexander Mak/Shutterstock, p17 matka_Wariatka/Shutterstock, p18 cheapbooks/Shutterstock, p19 Monkey Business Images/Shutterstock, p20 Antonio Guillem/Shutterstock, p21 karelnoppe/Shutterstock, p23 Trinity Mirror/Mirrorpix/Alamy Stock Photo, p24 l Joel Ginsburg/WENN.com/Alamy Stock Photo, p24 r KEITH MAYHEW/Alamy Stock Photo, p25 Action Plus Sports Images/Alamy Stock Photo, p26 l Image Source/Alamy Stock Photo, p26 c Mettus/Shutterstock, p26 r Maxim Blinkov/Shutterstock, p27 YAKOBCHUK VIACHESLAV/Shutterstock, p28 Roger Askew/Alamy Stock Photo, p29 pixelheadphoto digitalskillet/Shutterstock, p31 Monkey Business Images/Shutterstock, p32 l Cultura RM/Alamy Stock Photo, p32 r Halfpoint/Shutterstock, p34 © Crown copyright 2018, p37 Monkey Business Images/Shutterstock, p39 suriyachan/Shutterstock, p40 Bikeworldtravel/Shutterstock, p43 Daisy Daisy/Shutterstock, p45 Olimpik/Shutterstock, p46 MBI/Alamy Stock Photo, p47 Rawpixel.com/Shutterstock, p48 GagliardiImages/Shutterstock, p50 Iakov Filimonov/Shutterstock, p53 SpeedKingz/Shutterstock, p54 Oleg Golovnev/Shutterstock, p55 fizkes/Shutterstock, p56 bluezace/Shutterstock, p59 Tinseltown/Shutterstock, p60 Roger Utting/Shutterstock, pp62–63 LezinAV/Shutterstock, p64 Syda Productions/Shutterstock, p65 i viewfinder/Shutterstock, p67 Szasz-Fabian Jozsef/Shutterstock, p68 Wanwisspaul/Shutterstock, p70 violetblue/Shutterstock, p71 Peter Gudella/Shutterstock, p72 Jacek Chabraszewski/Shutterstock, p75 Jaren Jai Wicklund/Shutterstock, p76 Monkey Business Images/Shutterstock, p79 Roman Bodnarchuk/Shutterstock, p80 wavebreakmedia/Shutterstock, p82 Jeanette Teare/Shutterstock, p83 Hero Images Inc./Alamy Stock Photo, p84 Doucefleur/Shutterstock, p86 PhotoAlto/Alamy Stock Photo, p87 Sasa Prudkov/Shutterstock, p89 Iryna Tiumentseva/Shutterstock, p91 Monkey Business Images/Shutterstock, p92 Antonio Guillem/Shutterstock, p94 EdBockStock/Shutterstock, p95 stockerman/Shutterstock, p97 Blamb/Shutterstock.

Texts

We are grateful to the following for permission to reproduce copyright material:

An extract on p.40 from *The Girl Guide* by Mahara Ibrahim, pp.192-193, published by Frances Lincoln Children's Books, an imprint of The Quarto Group, copyright © 2017. Reproduced by permission of Quarto Publishing Plc; An extract on p.54 from *The Girls' Guide to Growing Up Great* by Sophie Elkan, copyright © Sophie Elkan, 2018. Reproduced by Green Tree, an imprint of Bloomsbury Publishing Plc; Extracts on p.70 about Teenagers and sleep, 2015, https://www.nutrition.org.uk/healthyliving/lifestages/teenagers.html, copyright © British Nutrition Foundation. Reproduced with permission; Extracts on p.74 from "Exercise and mental health: for young people", https://www.rcpsych.ac.uk/mental-health/parents-and-young-people/young-people/exercise-and-mental-health-for-young-people, copyright © March 2017, Royal College of Psychiatrists; An extract on p.75 from "Sleep and tiredness", https://www.nhs.uk/live-well/sleep-and-tiredness/why-are-teens-always-tired/, 2018 © Crown copyright; and An extract on p.80 from "How to tell kids about divorce: An age-by-age guide" by John Hoffman, originally published in *Todays Parent*, https://www.todaysparent.com/family/kids-and-divorce-an-age-by-age-guide, copyright © John Hoffman. Reproduced with kind permission.

Every effort has been made to trace the copyright holders and obtain permission to reproduce material in this book. Please do get in touch with any enquiries or any information.